COLLINS POCKET REFERENCE

ETIQUETTE

Adriana Hunter

D1079425

HarperCollins*Publishers*

HarperCollins Publishers
P.O. Box, Glasgow G4 0NB
www.fireandwater.com

First published 1997

Reprint 10 9 8 7 6 5

ISBN 0 00 472149 7

A catalogue record for this book is available from the British Library

Printed and bound in Great Britain by
Caledonian International Book Manufacturing, Glasgow

CONTENTS

INTRODUCTION

'Manners maketh man' is the school motto of one of Britain's oldest public schools. The development and adherence to a code of acceptable and expected social behaviour is an essential part of what makes us civilized. Throughout history, from the very earliest times, all cultures have had sophisticated codes of behaviour, defining in detail acceptable and unacceptable social practices and manners.

The distant, rudimentary origins of etiquette must have been similar to the unwritten rules that govern the behaviour of other animals. Almost all creatures have certain, clearly defined patterns of behaviour, which are an integral part of the continuing success of the species; for example, the ritualized behaviour required in animal 'courtship'. Also, animals that live in social groups have a distinct hierarchy of power: all the individuals may show deference to a leading patriarch or matriarch, and the young will show deference to adult members of the group.

Similar simple codes must surely have been the basis of human etiquette. These codes, or conventions, were developed over thousands of years to safeguard the survival of each species. Because humankind is more intelligent than the other creatures, it was, therefore, inevitable that these crude conventions developed into the increasingly complex rules of etiquette required for sophisticated social structures.

In the past etiquette became an overweening restriction on self-expression, for example in the ascetic (and unrealistic) representation of courtly love during the Middle Ages, and in the rigorous restraint on natural emotion expected in Victorian, middle-class families. Happily, in the 20th century the rules of etiquette have relaxed considerably, the edges have been smoothed off, there is greater allowance for individuality and

INTRODUCTION

greater tolerance. Rather than being a collection of strict rules to which everyone is expected to adhere, etiquette could now be defined as an unwritten code of correct and acceptable behaviour.

The purpose of good manners is for all forms of social contact to run smoothly; if we treat others as we would have them treat us, our interactions with other people should be easier and more pleasurable. Many rules of etiquette are born out of a need for simple courtesy, others are based on purely practical considerations, and yet others on a combination of the two.

A good example of the latter is the basic rule that you should not put your elbows on the table during a meal. If you do put your elbows on the table, you will probably lean forward on them: by doing this you might tip the table – a practical consideration – and you will almost certainly make it impossible for those on either side of you to speak to each other – which would be discourteous.

Etiquette is often described as an unwritten code because many of us learn the basics of good manners from our parents and are, therefore, equipped to deal with most situations. But all of us occasionally need to check up on things we have learned: it is not always easy to remember how to address an envelope to a divorced woman, for example, or how to lay a table for a dinner party.

On the other hand, we are sometimes thrown into situations for which we have not been prepared: for example, we do not frequently have to attend funerals and may need some guidance on what to wear and what to expect; neither do most people meet royalty every day of the week, so if they do meet a member of the royal family they need to know what to say and how to behave.

The **Collins Pocket Reference Etiquette** is intended to help you with just these kinds of queries. It is a simple and easy-to-use guide to etiquette for everyday and special occasions. Over and above all the information provided, there are two important rules of etiquette that should always be remembered: (1) if you are unsure of what to do or how to behave you should check with someone else, or watch what those around you are doing (this advice is frequently repeated in the book); (2) if you realize that you are doing something wrong, do it with conviction and others may not even notice your slip (this is not so easy to observe because it calls for a certain amount courage).

This guide is laid out in three sections to make it easier to use. The first section covers (in alphabetical order) the **Basic Rules** of etiquette; it tells you how to deal with everyday circumstances, outlining, for example, good table manners, how much you should tip people, and how to behave in the office. Each of these areas is divided into subheadings so that it is easy for you to find the information you need.

The second section deals with **Special Occasions** (also in alphabetical order); covering christenings and parties, and the more difficult occasions such as funerals and visiting the sick. It explains, for example, how to organize a dinner party and how to be a good guest at one, how to behave in an interview and what to do when you are invited to the theatre. Again each of these areas is dealt with under a number of subheadings.

The final section of the book is a quick-reference A to Z section of material not dealt with in the rest of the book, plus a résumé on some of the topics covered in the first two sections. This makes it easier for you to find the precise piece of information you need; for instance, if you want to know how to lay the cutlery for a dinner party, but don't want to read through the whole dinner parties section, just look up **cutlery** in the A to Z section.

Many of the entries in the A to Z section may refer you to other parts of the book where you will be able to find more

INTRODUCTION

information on the subject. Or if the subject is too large to be covered at all in the A to Z section, the entry will indicate how to find the relevant information in the first two sections of the book. In these cases the entry will just say 'see . . .' or 'see also . . .'. Or you may be referred to another entry in the A to Z.

Finally, at the end of the book there is a table of titles and forms of address. This table lists members of the royal family, the aristocracy, government ministers, church dignitaries, legal dignitaries, and local government and civic officials. In each instance the table tells you how to address the individual in person, how to address an envelope to him or her and what title or name to use at the opening of a letter to him or her.

CHILDREN

Many people are so wrapped up in their children that they forget that not everyone will find them quite so irresistible. Parents should avoid spending the whole time talking about their children, and they should never assume that their children are automatically invited out with them. If your children's names are not mentioned on an invitation, but you would particularly like to take them with you, ask your hosts whether you can bring them with you. Try to phrase the question so that your host can say no, rather than saying, 'You don't mind if I bring the children, do you?'.

Babies and toddlers

As with children of all ages, parents should not assume that their babies are invited everywhere with them, or that other people are dying to see them. If you take a baby somewhere with you, do it discreetly so that you don't break up the whole party, and don't breast-feed in front of other people unless you are sure that they won't mind.

Toddlers are not very well coordinated and are notoriously inquisitive: if you take them into a shop or someone else's home, they could easily damage valuables. Take a favourite toy of theirs with you to keep them distracted. Try to anticipate potential accidents, and avoid them – if necessary – by moving tempting valuables out of reach. If your child does damage something, you should offer to mend or replace it.

Other people's babies

Parents are inevitably proud of their babies, so it is polite and flattering to talk about them. Try to be tolerant about a baby's crying, demands and smells. If you have asked parents to bring little ones with them, provide some sort of facilities for them: a separate bathroom, a few toys and some children's drinks. If you have house guests who bring a baby, ask the mother in advance what she will need while she is staying.

Children's manners

There are three basic rules for trying to ensure that children have good manners in company: their parents should set a good example; children should be taught manners and disciplined at home; they should be introduced to other people at an early age, so that they learn to interact with strangers.

If your children are familiar with the basics of manners at home, you won't have embarrassing confrontations with them when you take them somewhere else. Children should be able to eat a meal with adults, but if the meal drags on, parents should ask their hosts if their children can leave the table early.

Children should learn at an early age how to be introduced to people and how to reply to adults' questions. But they should not be allowed to dominate a conversation by interrupting and assuming that everyone will listen.

If your children do misbehave in front of other people, don't be afraid to tick them off: your friends will respect you far more if you try to correct them than if you let them continue to drive everyone mad! On the other hand, if you see a tantrum brewing, do everything you can to deflect it and do not resort to arguing with or spanking your child in front of others. Many people – however misguidedly – will sympathize with the child, and children are wily enough to recognize and exploit this sympathy.

Other people's children

Don't be shy about talking to children, and try not to patronize them when you talk to them. The more natural your questions, the more likely a child is to open up and reply. If someone else's child misbehaves in front of his or her parents, you should leave it up to the parents to discipline their child. But if you are looking after someone else's child and it misbehaves, you should tell the child that they are being naughty. This is especially true if you have children of your own: your own children will not find it fair if their guest is allowed to do things that they are forbidden.

Children in public places

If you take children to large functions or on public transport, always ensure that you have everything you need with you: a change of nappies if necessary, something for the child to eat and drink, possibly a change of clothes, and something to keep them occupied. If your child cries or becomes noisy at an inconvenient moment, don't waste time trying to keep them quiet: take them outside as quickly as possible. The most common example of this is when babies cry during wedding ceremonies: this is totally unacceptable, and the screaming youngster should be taken outside immediately.

Children's parties

When planning a children's party, you should make sure you have enough activities organized to keep the children busy. Check also that the venue you choose is suitable, and move any valuables out of the way. Don't invite too wide an age-group of children and make sure that you will have enough adults present to cope with feeding the children, organizing their games and checking how recently each child has been to the toilet!

Make it clear on the invitation whether the children will be inside or outside during the party so that parents know how to dress them. Bear in mind the safety problems that can arise

BASIC RULES

when youngsters come in contact with candles and kettles of boiling water.

The children themselves should be involved in the 'administration' of the party. The host children should help with the invitations and all the arrangements; and the young guests should be involved in replying to their invitations and thanking for the party. It is never too early to learn these social skills.

CHILDREN – CHECKLIST

Important dos and don'ts

✓ **DO teach your children good manners early**
✓ **DO ask before taking your children with you to a friend's house**
✓ **DO take toys, clothes and food for your child with you**
✗ **DON'T let your child interrupt adult conversations**
✗ **DON'T scold other people's children if their parents are with them**
✗ **DON'T let your child ruin someone's wedding with its screaming**

CORRECT CLOTHES

The safest way to ensure that you are wearing the correct clothes is to check with someone else. You will generally feel more comfortable if you are slightly underdressed than overdressed, but if you are very underdressed this may appear as a snub to your hosts. Invitations to most occasions will indicate what the man should wear; outlined below are the unofficial 'rules' about what a woman should wear in each instance.

Black tie

This traditionally refers to a man's black dinner suit – a matching black jacket and trousers, often trimmed with satin – worn with a white shirt and black bow tie. Nowadays, ironically, the tie is often anything but black. Amusing bow ties are often worn with matching cummerbunds or with equally gaudy waistcoats. In summer or warm climates, white tuxedos may be worn in the place of dinner jackets. Black tie is worn to dances, smart dinners and some weddings.

The corresponding women's clothes vary according to the occasion: from a short, smart dress or suit for a dinner or a wedding, to a 'ballerina-length' (mid-calf) ball gown for a dance. The key is to be smart in accordance with the formality of the man's dinner suit.

White tie

Invitations to formal balls and royal or diplomatic functions may stipulate this increasingly rare outfit, which comprises black tail coat and trousers, a stiff-fronted shirt with a wing collar and studs, and a matching white bow tie and waistcoat.

BASIC RULES

White-tie functions give women the opportunity to push the boat out with lavish, full-length dresses or skirts. Gloves – which should be removed only for eating – and elaborate jewellery are also appropriate. If the function does not include dancing, women are expected to be more 'covered up'. Off-the-shoulder gowns are suitable for white-tie occasions that incorporate dancing.

Morning dress
A day in the Royal Enclosure at Ascot or a formal wedding could call for morning dress: a black or grey tail coat worn with matching trousers, a waistcoat, stiff-collared shirt and top hat. A grey cravat can be substituted for a tie with morning dress.

Ladies should be dressed elegantly: anything from a chic tailored suit to a smart, floaty dress, preferably with a hat (at the Royal Enclosure the crown of the head must be covered).

Lounge suit
Lounge suits are worn by men for many different occasions: work, job interviews, parties, weddings, christenings and funerals. For more formal occasions, darker coloured suits are more appropriate, and suit jackets should not be removed. Women's clothes for the same occasions can vary enormously, but they should reflect the fact that a suit is a smart form of dress. Some places that stipulate that men should wear suits will not accept ladies wearing trousers or culottes, however smart.

Jacket and tie
Some parties or outings may call for something more than casual but less than a suit. The safest option for a man is to wear a blazer or sports jacket with a tie. Women may wear anything so long as it takes into account the fact that the men are sufficiently formal to be wearing ties.

Special occasions

Although first nights and charity performances may stipulate black tie, most outings to the opera, ballet or theatre are no longer very formal. What people choose to wear usually depends on who they are going with and how much they paid for their tickets.

Glyndebourne is an exception: part of the pleasure of attending opera performances at Glyndebourne is to have a picnic in evening dress (but be sure you have a raincoat in the back of the car). The Royal Enclosure at Ascot requires morning dress for men and formal wear, including a hat, for women. The Stewards' Enclosure at Henley Royal Regatta requires men to wear a jacket or blazer, which they must never remove; women are not permitted to enter the enclosure if they are wearing trousers, denim, culottes or above knee-length skirts.

Optional extras

Both men and women may wear jewellery, although it is still less acceptable for men to do so. More lavish jewellery is appropriate for evening functions but inappropriate for work and job inter-

---

CORRECT CLOTHES – CHECKLIST

Important dos and don'ts

✓ **DO check with your hosts or other guests if in doubt what to wear**
✓ **DO dress to match the formality of the man's clothes**
✗ **DON'T overdress for anything but the most formal occasions**

---

views, and tactless at funerals. Hats can be worn by men and women at any time; a woman should keep a hat on when going inside, whereas a man should remove his (unless entering a synagogue). Men should raise their hats as a sign of respect when introduced to a lady. Veils can be an attractive addition to hats for women, but they are not always practical: at weddings they may interfere with eating and drinking, and at funerals they may make it difficult to wipe tears away. Furs are becoming increasingly unacceptable, and many people are uninhibited when criticizing others for wearing them.

See also **Scottish Formal Dress** in the A to Z section.

CORRECT GIFTS

Whether a gift is a sign of love or a token of gratitude try to make sure that it is appropriate: if you go to stay with someone who has just moved house, give him or her something useful or attractive for the household; if you visit a friend who has just given birth, give her something for the baby. When you are invited out for a meal, you are not expected to take a present, but many guests like to take chocolates or flowers.

Birthday presents are often difficult; try to make presents relevant to the person's interests and hobbies. Wedding presents are sometimes the easiest because so many couples have wedding lists (see **Weddings**). Unless you know the couple especially well and are sure they will like something you have chosen for them, it is safest to choose a present from their list: this will avoid embarrassing doubling up of presents, and will ensure they get the things they need for their new life. Whoever you are buying a present for, remember that it is always best to get something small and appropriate. See also, in the Special Occasions section, **Christenings** and **Christmas Cards and Presents**.

DIVORCE

Divorce is one of the most awkward and emotionally painful situations. Divorces are not only difficult for the partners involved but for those around them, and divorce proceedings should be kept as civil and as private as possible.

Making arrangements

In divorce agreements, both partners should strive to be reasonable and to accept some degree of compromise. Protracted arguing over property, belongings and children will only increase the bitterness and may be extremely damaging to the children. Even if you never want to see your ex again, try to be civil for the sake of others if you meet him or her by chance; and, if you have children, try to keep in touch with your in-laws for the children's sake.

A friend in need

Friends can be a great help at such a difficult time. Don't assume your friends will know that you have divorced, let them know by dropping them a little note. It is especially important to contact adults, such as teachers, who see your children regularly.

If you know a couple who have recently been divorced, offer them your friendship and support. If their break up was acrimonious, it is virtually impossible to stay in touch with both partners: you will seem disloyal and may end up losing both of them.

Marrying again

Remarriage is acceptable after the decree absolute has been issued, but the Church of England will offer only a service of blessing and not a full marriage service to divorcés. If you have very young children they may accept your new partner as mother or father, although this may cause hurtful complications with their true parent. In most cases it is best to use the first name of their stepfather or stepmother.

DRIVER'S ETIQUETTE

Driver's etiquette should be a combination of common sense and respect for the highway code. Its principal aim is to make sure that the roads are safe to use.

Thinking of others

In all situations, we should be considerate towards other road users. If the left side of the road is obstructed, for example, with parked cars, drivers should wait for a break in the oncoming traffic, rather than launching out into the right side of the road and forcing the other traffic to wait. When traffic is amassing in a side road, it will only add a matter of seconds to your journey time if you let the first car onto the main road in front of you. Let other road users know what manoeuvre you are planning to do: indicate or, if necessary, signal with your hands.

The single most important element of driver's etiquette is the thank you: a simple wave of your hand in your rear-view mirror will let fellow drivers know that you appreciate the fact that they have waited for you or let you into the traffic. The more people thank each other on the roads, the more inclined we all feel to oblige other drivers.

Avoiding confrontations

However late or frustrated you are, you should always try to avoid provoking other drivers: don't steal a parking space that someone else was obviously about to use, don't overtake a car and then slow right down, and don't cut in front of another car so that it is forced to slow down.

If another driver provokes you, try to keep your cool; if you rise to the bait you are giving exactly the desired reaction and you may lose concentration, which is dangerous.

FRIENDS AND ETIQUETTE

In order to keep our friends we have to observe a few courtesies towards them. Always remember this simple formula: treat your friends as you would have them treat you. You shouldn't invade your friends' lives and press yourself on them, nor should you abandon them because you are carried away by a new love affair or job. Be considerate towards your friends and contribute by paying for your share of rounds of drinks and splitting the cost of outings.

Sharing a flat

Living with people requires a degree of thoughtfulness and consideration, and perhaps even a certain amount of reasonable compromise. Whether you share accommodation with an old friend or with people you only met when you moved in, there will be times when you find their habits, their friends or their untidiness irritating. The best way to deal with minor irritations is to ignore them. If there is something that your flatmate does regularly that really annoys you – like spending hours in the bathroom every morning – it's best to be frank and discuss the problem openly.

It is important to respect a flatmate's privacy and property: knock before going into his or her own room, and never use his or her belongings without asking. Two people will usually have different ideas about tidiness, so try to sort out in advance who is responsible for which chores around the flat.

Some of the most awkward problems between flatmates may arise over telephone bills; the easiest way to deal with this tricky issue is to make a note of each of your calls and to ask for an itemized bill.

INTRODUCTIONS

Many people are nervous about introductions, probably because they are so important. The ability to introduce people is a special art. When making introductions most people use first names as well as surnames. Older people may prefer to be introduced by their surnames only, and surnames may be used at formal or business meetings.

It is polite, and often a help to conversation, to give a person's rank or title when introducing them. If you are introducing two people together it helps if you at least hint at the relationship between them, explaining whether they are brother and sister, recently engaged, just friends or colleagues.

It is always polite to introduce people who do not know each other, whatever the circumstances. For example, if you are walking along the street with a friend and you bump into someone you know, don't just chat with them and then walk on without introducing them to the person you are with.

The good host
As a host you should avoid introducing a newcomer to a great circle of people all at once; he or she will never remember all the names. Neither should you give just the names and hope people will get on with each other. Try to give your guests some information about each other so that they can begin a conversation. Ideally, you should help them begin a conversation before flitting off to attend to other duties.

If you see anyone on their own, scoop them up quickly and introduce them to someone. If a friend's name slips out of your head at the vital moment, you may just have to admit to it. Most people will understand – it happens to everyone at some time.

Being introduced

When you are introduced to someone, you will remember their name more easily if you make eye contact, repeat their name immediately and try to associate their name with some characteristic of theirs, such as his or her hair colour, clothes or way of speaking.

If you forget someone's name, apologize and ask him or her what it is. But then you must really listen and make an effort to remember the name, because it would be rude to ask again. If you feel the person you have been introduced to deserves your respect use their surname until they invite you to use their first name. If you are offered a hand to shake or even a cheek to kiss, you should reciprocate.

It is sometimes embarrassing if someone recognizes you but you don't remember them; it is safest to play along until you remember them or can say with certitude, 'I don't think we've met before'.

There are times when you may find yourself on your own in a room full of people; you must be courageous and introduce yourself to someone or ask a friend to make some introductions for you. If you go on to introduce the person you are with to someone else, try to use the same 'format' that was used when they were introduced to you; this is especially important if the person has some kind of title.

Nobility and dignitaries

You should never introduce yourself to royalty, but wait to be introduced. If you want to introduce someone else to them, use the format 'may I introduce my wife, sir'. You should address them initially as 'Your Royal Highness' (or 'Your Majesty' for the Queen) and subsequently as 'sir' or 'ma'am'. Dukes and Duchesses are addressed as 'your grace', and other nobles are addressed as 'Lord' or 'sir' and 'Lady'. Ambassadors are addressed as 'ambassador' and referred to as 'his excellency'; senior clergymen may be 'your grace'(if a bishop), 'your lord-ship' or 'your eminence'(if a cardinal). If in doubt, it is usually safest to revert to 'sir'. See the **Forms of Address** section at the end of the book.

INTRODUCTIONS – CHECKLIST

Important dos and don'ts

✓ **DO tell people something about each other to help them start a conversation**
✓ **DO use a person's name as soon as you have been introduced**
✓ **DO let someone know if you didn't catch their name**
✗ **DON'T introduce too many people at once**
✗ **DON'T expect guests to introduce themselves**
✗ **DON'T ignore an outstretched hand, shake it**

LETTER WRITING

Although telephone conversations have to some extent superseded the letter, letters are still an important way of communicating. They allow you to lay out information clearly and in your own time, they show more respect for the correspondent than a quick telephone call, and they can remain as a physical record of communication. Letters should be written promptly, preferably within a week of the event or letter to which they refer.

Starting a letter

Before you write a letter, think what sort of paper you should use. If you are writing to a friend the choice is yours, but if the letter is at all formal or if it is a business letter you should use a good size sheet of white, cream or pale blue paper. Business letters should be typed whenever possible – typing is clearer than handwriting – or written in black or blue ink. Typed letters are acceptable in most circumstances, although intimate letters and letters of sympathy or thanks seem more sincere if they are handwritten.

All letters should carry your address and the date; business letters should also include the addressee's name and address as well as any reference numbers. The text of the letter should begin a little way down the page, usually about a third of the way down, and it should have a margin to either side, rather than filling the whole width of the page.

Addressing your correspondent

Almost all letters begin with the word 'Dear'. If you don't know the correspondent's name and cannot discover it, put 'Dear sir or madam'. Wherever possible, find out their name – even if this means ringing to ask – and check whether a woman likes to be addressed as Miss, Mrs or Ms.

Doctors, professors and people with a rank in the services usually like to be addressed as such in a letter. For the forms of address used for the nobility, religious dignitaries and government officials, see the **Forms of Address** section at the end of the book.

Business letters

An effective business letter is short and to the point, ideally using only one sheet of paper. If two or more pages are used, number the pages clearly and, preferably, reiterate the date and reference number on each page. Avoid very formal language: you may confuse yourself and your correspondent.

Letters of application should explain briefly how you know the post is vacant: you may, for example, be replying to a newspaper advertisement or following up a tip from someone within the company. You should explain clearly and honestly why you think you would be suitable for the post, and give relevant 'highlights' from your curriculum vitae, which should be enclosed.

If you enclose material in a business letter, put the letters 'Enc.' after signing your name at the end. If you are sending copies of the letter to other people, put the letters 'cc' at the end with a list of their names. Type or print your name, preferred title and – if relevant – position under your signature (unless these appear in your letterhead), so that your correspondent does not have to guess at your name from your signature when he or she replies to your letter. If you are signing a letter on behalf of the person whose details are printed at the foot of the letter, put the letters 'pp' (abbreviation of the Latin phrase *per procurationem*, 'on behalf of') in front of their name. Always keep a copy of business letters and make a copy of any material sent with them.

If you are applying for jobs and using a referee's name frequently, you should let your referee know all the companies who have been given his or her name and address. Letters of reference should be relevant and truthful. If you really cannot recommend the candidate it is better to refuse to write the letter than to lie.

Thank-you letters

Telephone calls are acceptable as thanks only for the most informal occasions. Postcards are also acceptable for smaller occasions, but a gift or larger function deserves a letter. Thank-you letters should be written promptly; they need not be long but should feel sincere and enthusiastic. The letter need not deal only with the thing you are thanking for, you may want to include some news about yourself, but it is polite to reiterate your thanks at the end of the letter. If a thank-you letter for a party or meal is sent to a couple, it is usually addressed to the wife alone, as the hostess is traditionally considered to be responsible for entertaining. If you are sent money you should always send a letter of thanks as this also acts as a receipt.

Complaint, condolence and sympathy

Letters of condolence and sympathy are often the most difficult but they are worthwhile: they are a great comfort. Always tell your correspondent that they need not thank you for your letter of sympathy or condolence, because this relieves them of a burdensome duty at a time of unhappiness; on the other hand, it will not stop them from replying if they would like to. Many people who are ill or have recently been bereaved feel lonely and are not sure how to use their time, they will very much appreciate a letter and may take pleasure in replying. If you receive letters of sympathy and feel unable to reply to them, try to find someone who can send a note on your behalf or have some little cards of thanks printed.

Letters of apology and complaint are also difficult to write. Letters of apology should be written as soon as possible, whereas letters of complaint are best left until your anger has had a chance to cool. In both cases, try to be clear and succinct. This will be more effective than a rambling, emotive letter.

Replying to formal invitations

When replying to formal invitations you should refer to yourself in the third person, for example: 'Mr James Liddle thanks Mrs Peter Cordon for her kind invitation to . . .', then follow the precise wording of the invitation, including details of time and place. At the end put a comma and say either 'and has great pleasure in accepting', or 'and very much regrets that he is unable to accept'. If you can not accept an invitation, explain briefly why not. Even if you simply say 'due to a prior engagement' this will reassure your hosts that you are not just turning down their invitation.

Ending a letter

Most formal letters end with 'Yours sincerely' or with the more formal 'Yours faithfully'. The latter should always be used if you do not know the name of your correspondent. It is now acceptable in regular business correspondence to use the less formal 'best wishes' or 'best regards'.

Letters to Royalty, ambassadors and eminent judges should end 'I have the honour to be your most humble and obedient servant.' The way that you end personal letters is entirely up to you.

The envelope

A letter should be folded a minimum of times before it is put in an envelope, and ideally it should fit the envelope well. The stamp should be positioned near the top right-hand corner of the envelope, and the address should be about half way down towards the left-hand margin so that it is not obscured by the postmark. If you know the postcode always use it as part of the address. If you are sending a letter abroad or sending a parcel, put the letters 'Exp' (from the French word *expéditeur* – 'sender') followed by your own name and address on the back.

When addressing a letter to a man use either Mr, his title or his rank. Some people use 'Esq' after a man's name, as a sign of respect, for example, 'Edward Mallard, Esq'. But 'Esq' cannot be combined with Mr or any other title. If a person has honours, it is a sign of respect to add the letters after his or her name on an

---

LETTER WRITING – CHECKLIST

Important dos and don'ts

✓ **DO put your full address and the correct date on every letter**
✓ **DO check your correspondent's name and title**
✓ **DO write promptly**
✗ **DON'T use a referee's name without letting them know**
✗ **DON'T reply to a business letter without using reference numbers (if provided)**
✗ **DON'T telephone when a letter would be more appropriate**

---

envelope. For security reasons, many people in the services no longer like their rank to be used on envelopes.

Addressing letters to a woman is more difficult: a woman may be Miss, Mrs, Ms or she may have some form of title – try to check before writing. Traditionally a married or widowed woman is addressed using her husband's name, for example Mrs John Carmichael; and a divorcée uses her own name, for example Mrs Sheila Carmichael. Many women now prefer to be addressed using their own name even if they are married, and some professional women still use their maiden names for business purposes even after they are married.

OFFICE ETIQUETTE

A large percentage of most of people's waking hours are spent at work, and that time will be spent far more pleasantly if they and their colleagues observe a few simple courtesies towards each other.

Newcomers

When a new person joins a company he or she should be introduced to immediate colleagues as well as the head of department. Newcomers should be given a clear idea of everyone's specific job – and of where their own jobs fit into that structure. They should not be kept in the dark about everyday things such as where the lavatories are and how to get a cup of coffee.

If you start a new job and feel you haven't been told enough, ask your colleagues, it will help you get to know them.

Respecting the company

If you are a good employee you should respect the company you work for, and you should be a good representative for the company in your contact with other people. You should be polite and helpful with any visitors, and you should ensure that they are offered something to drink if they are kept waiting. Your telephone manner should be equally courteous and helpful (see

You should not exploit the company by systematically arriving late, leaving early, taking long lunch hours, asking for extra time off or failing to do your share of chores. Neither should you exploit the facilities by taking stationery or blocking the telephone lines with your personal calls.

BASIC RULES

Working together
In order for people to work well together each employee must know his or her own role within the company, and the relationships between all employees must be based on mutual respect. Those in senior positions should be firm but not imperious with their staff, delegating justly according to each person's abilities and work schedule. Junior employees should treat their seniors with deference, without simpering, in order to maintain the structure of the company.

Talking to each other
At all levels, people should communicate with each other: when you ask someone to do something be precise, don't expect them to know automatically what you want. If you are asked to do something and are not sure that you have understood, it is always better to ask than to spend a long time doing the job incorrectly.

You should also talk to your colleagues about more general things; your working atmosphere will be more pleasant if you are on friendly terms with them. But you should not talk so much that you detract from your own and colleagues' work, and you should avoid talking at length about your personal life.

Further intimacy
Sexual intimacy between people who work together is not recommended; indeed, in some companies it is a sackable offence. It strains working relationships and can damage careers. If you are irresistibly drawn to someone at work, you should think seriously about the consequences before succumbing to his or her charms.

The suggestion of sexual intimacy can be equally disturbing in the work place. If something you say or do seems to upset or offend a colleague, you should respect his or her wishes and stop immediately. If you are the 'victim' of such comments or actions, confront the person who is upsetting you. Let the offending person know that you do not like what he or she is doing, and warn him or her that you will speak to someone else within the company if you have to.

OFFICE ETIQUETTE – CHECKLIST

Important dos and don'ts

√ **DO respect the people you work with**
√ **DO ask if you're not sure what is wanted of you**
√ **DO chip in with office chores**
X **DON'T make too many personal calls**
X **DON'T make a habit of arriving late**
X **DON'T keep things bottled up if something or someone is upsetting you**

PETS

Pets are rather like children: our own are delightful, other people's can be intolerable or even frightening. However, never consider your pets before your guests.

Guidelines

Dogs should not be allowed to intimidate guests with their barking and jumping up; if you have a noisy dog, shut it in another room before opening the front door.

Pet owners should always ask before taking their pets to someone else's house. Once there, the pet should be kept well disciplined and any 'mistakes' should be cleared up immediately by the profusely apologetic owner. Pets should not be allowed onto other people's furniture even if they are allowed to do this at home.

You should never shy away from saying that you don't like or are allergic to animals; owners should respect this and take their pets away. Tell owners if you don't want their pets on your furniture or even in your house.

On the other hand, you may love all sorts of animals, but it is not a good idea to be over familiar with someone else's pet unless you know it well: boisterous games and teasing may irritate an animal, and could end in tears. You should never feed a pet titbits without asking its owner; many owners do not like their pets to learn to beg, and just one kindly meant titbit might teach the animal to beg from other guests.

ROMANCE

Although the intricate rules of chivalry no longer govern romance, there are still some key courtesies that can make relationships between men and women easier and more enjoyable. Couples should, however, not think only of themselves – they should consider those around them: it can be very tiresome for other people if a couple is involved in kissing, petting or simply flirting in public. Furthermore, lovers should not abandon their friends for the sake of a relationship: friendships usually last longer than romantic attachments.

Making a date

When two people have met and enjoyed each other's company, it is perfectly acceptable for the man or the women to contact the other and suggest meeting again. It is best if the caller suggests a specific reason for meeting – such as a meal or a theatre trip – rather than just saying 'can I see you?'. This makes it easier for both partners to know what to expect and what to wear.

If you are invited out by someone you really would rather not see again, refuse the invitation as diplomatically as possible and continue to refuse further offers without suggesting alternative dates that would suit you. Eventually, the caller should realize that you don't want to see him or her again. If you are doing the inviting you should not put too much pressure on the other person; certainly don't resort to saying 'well, when are you free then?', so that they are forced to name a day or to say outright that they do not want to see you again. If someone appears to be evasive but would genuinely like to see you again, he or she will suggest an alternative date. Even after a first date, one partner should not barrage the other with invitations: if someone really likes you, he or she will find time to call you.

The first date

When a man invites a woman on the first date he should pick her up or – in any event – be sure to reach the rendezvous early so that the woman does not have to wait for him. If a man invites a woman out for a meal or to the theatre the woman is under no obligation to offer to pay, although many women like to contribute. It is, however, rude to argue over paying if the person who instigated the outing has insisted. Some women like to 'go Dutch' so that they do not feel indebted to the man or under any pressure to sleep with him. However, if the man has insisted on paying, a woman should not feel threatened by this; nowhere is there any code that says men can expect sexual favours from women for whom they have bought a meal.

At the end of the date, the man should accompany the woman home and should check that she gets through the front door safely. If the woman asks the man in, this is often interpreted as a sexual invitation: if it was not intended that way, the woman should make that very clear.

Etiquette and sex

There are two very important things to remember about sex: first, that it is illegal to force someone to have sex, and second, that both partners should discuss and be in agreement about contraception. In order to protect themselves from AIDS and other sexually transmitted diseases, couples who have not known each other long should use a condom. It is acceptable and even common for girls to carry condoms now, and many girls will say that they are not on the pill, even if they are, and invite their partner to use a condom. It is important that everyone, man or woman, should have a responsible attitude towards contraception, and not assume that their partner has taken precautions.

During or after sex it is cruel to criticize a lover's performance, especially if he or she asks you about it, as this is a sign of insecurity. If you have to leave shortly after making love, do not do so abruptly and make it clear whether you would like to see the other person again. Ideally, couples should know in advance whether they are embarking on what could be a long-term relationship or simply a one-off encounter. If you do not intend to get involved with someone, you may hurt him or her more by getting in touch again after a one night stand. But if you are truly smitten by someone, he or she may be touched if you send a small gift the following day as a sign of your affection and esteem.

Saying goodbye

The end of a relationship is very difficult for both partners. The person who is instigating the break up should try to do it as

---

ROMANCE – CHECKLIST

Important dos and don'ts

✓ **DO let someone know you noticed them**
✓ **DO establish what you feel about each other before someone gets hurt**
✓ **DO talk about contraception before having sex**
✗ **DON'T bombard someone with invitations**
✗ **DON'T abandon your friends because you have a new lover**
✗ **DON'T kiss intimately in public**

BASIC RULES

quickly and gently as possible; if you keep trying to patch up differences or you haven't the courage to make a clean break, you only cause your partner additional pain. Wherever possible you should discuss a break up in person: a letter may appear cold and heartless, and a telephone call is lazy and offhand.

If your partner tells you he or she is leaving you, try not to argue or to beg your loved one to stay; this will only damage your pride further and may make you even more bitter about the break up.

SMOKING

Smoking is a source of pleasure and relaxation for a minority of the population and of misery and discomfort for the majority. It can, therefore, cause awkward confrontations and feelings of resentment. In the last ten years the number of people who smoke has fallen rapidly. Smoking in public has become less acceptable and many public places, such as restaurants and cinemas, as well as public transport, have banned smoking altogether.

Do you mind if I smoke?

Before lighting a cigarette, cigar or pipe, you should consider the circumstances carefully. If you are in a public place, you should check first for 'No Smoking' signs and, if applicable, move to a designated smoking area. Check also that there is an ashtray close at hand.

Always ask people with you or nearby whether they mind you smoking, especially if you are in a confined space or if anyone is eating. Asking other people whether they mind you smoking was once something of a formality, but nowadays non-smokers may well take the opportunity to tell you they would prefer you not to smoke. In this case, you should respect their wishes and, if possible, move somewhere else to smoke.

You should make a particular point of asking if you are in the home, office or car of a non-smoker. People who live in a smoke-free environment are especially sensitive to the lingering smell of tobacco smoke. It would be most discourteous to argue if they asked you not to smoke.

BASIC RULES

Even if you are outside and not actually with other people, your smoke can still inconvenience those near you. If you are in a crowd or walking along a street, smoke may be blown straight into the faces of other people, and you might even inadvertently burn someone.

When you are smoking

Once you have established that no-one minds you smoking, it is polite to offer cigarettes to your companions. It is also polite to offer a light to anyone with an unlit cigarette.

While you are smoking, try to keep your cigarette and its smoke away from other people. Turn your head away from people when you are exhaling smoke, and tip the ash off your cigarette regularly so that it does not fall.

If you light a cigarette without asking those near if they mind, you may find that someone objects strongly and asks you to put it out. In these circumstances it is best to avoid confrontation by extinguishing your cigarette or by moving away so that you are no longer inconveniencing him or her.

Non-smokers

It is increasingly common for non-smokers to ask friends or even strangers not to smoke, especially if they are eating or are in a confined space. If someone's cigarette smoke would genuinely inconvenience you, it is perfectly acceptable for you to ask him or her not to smoke, and they should respect your wishes. On the other hand, it would be unfair to deny them the pleasure of a cigarette simply because you disapprove of smoking.

If someone has lit a cigarette and you are finding it unpleasant, it is best to move away or quietly ask the smoker to extinguish the cigarette. You will achieve little by trying to wave the smoke away, and will only engender resentment if you make a fuss.

SMOKING – CHECKLIST

Important dos and don'ts

✓ **DO make sure you're not in a NO SMOKING area**
✓ **DO ask if people mind you smoking**
✓ **DO offer people cigarettes**
✓ **DON'T blow smoke into people's faces**
✓ **DON'T smoke while people are eating**
✓ **DON'T smoke if someone has expressly asked you not to**

SPORTING ETIQUETTE

Much of the so-called etiquette that we observe in sport revolves around the safety of the players, fair play and good sportsmanship. If you are not sure of the rules of any particular sport, check with a local club. Although games may be competitive – or, as with croquet, downright nasty – there are still parameters of courtesy that players are expected to respect.

Here are a few of the key rules of good sportsmanship: don't let your competitive spirit overshadow your enjoyment of the game; don't argue with other players about the validity of a shot or point; don't distract other players when they are concentrating; and always thank your partner and/or opponent after a game.

Tennis

Tennis is a popular and very social game because so many people know how to play it. But poor manners on the tennis court can easily damage friendships, even – or perhaps especially – in casual games without umpires. If the players are in any doubt about whether a ball was in or not, they should simply play the point again rather than arguing.

In doubles matches, partners should discuss whether they intend to work the sides of the court or the front and the back; once established, they should respect each other's 'territory' and apologize if they infringe on it.

Some tennis clubs or even the owners of private courts like players to wear full tennis whites on their courts. If you are joining a tennis club, going to a tennis party, or borrowing someone's court, check whether you should wear tennis whites.

Golf

The popularity of golf is rising rapidly, which means there are more and more people on courses. The few simple rules of golf etiquette should, therefore, be observed all the more closely. The most important rule in golf is to make sure that your shots do not endanger anyone: always check before you address the ball, and if in doubt call 'fore!' as a warning.

If you are holding up the players behind you on the course, let them pass however exciting your game is, and always leave the greens promptly to let other players onto them. Players are usually expected to make good any damage they do to the course and the greens as they go along. Finally, most golf courses have strict rules about dogs on the course, some do not allow dogs on the course at all. Whether you are playing golf and would like to take your dog or simply wanting to walk your dog on a golf course, always check with the club beforehand.

Sailing

Not many people have the opportunity to sail regularly, and those invited for a day's sailing may, therefore, leap at the chance. Before you go check what clothes and equipment you may need, let your host know if you are inclined to seasickness or if you can't swim, and try to learn a few useful words because sailing boats have a vocabulary all their own.

Hunting

The pressures of the anti-blood sports league have seen an increase in popularity for the non-blood sport, drag-hunting, and have not affected the strict codes of etiquette observed on the hunting field. When you arrive at a meet, you should greet the master 'Good morning, sir' regardless of the time of day. During the day's hunting you should never ride ahead of the master or interfere with hounds. If your horse refuses an obstacle you should circle out of the way as quickly as possible so as not to obstruct the rest of the field. At the end of the day you should bid the master farewell: 'Good evening, sir', again regardless of the time of day.

SPORTING ETIQUETTE – CHECKLIST

Important dos and don'ts

√ **DO play fair and keep to the spirit of the game**
√ **DO dress correctly, and check if in doubt**
X **DON'T put competitiveness before courtesy**
X **DON'T win or lose with bad grace**

SWEARING

Swearing is far more widespread now that it was just a generation ago, but it should still only be used in the company of those we know will tolerate it. It is unfair on parents to teach their children swearwords by swearing in front of them. It is also disrespectful to swear in front of the elderly whose earlier days were not so peppered with obscenities and blasphemies. Swearing is still less acceptable out of the mouths of women than of men; but whoever is driven to swearing by extremes of anger, frustration or pain should apologize for doing so. Those who address their abuse at another person are being very offensive and they should be prepared to suffer the consequences.

TABLE MANNERS

Good table manners form one of the cornerstones of etiquette. Fundamentally, they are the practical techniques for eating as easily and discreetly as possible; their object is for a person to be able to eat food from his or her plate without disturbing or embarrassing other people at the table. But there is much more to table manners than the way you eat: they include everything from sitting down at the beginning of a meal to leaving the table at the end.

Taking your seat

At a formal meal the guests should not sit down until their hostess and guest of honour are seated, or until they are invited to by their host. They should ensure they are in the correct seat and help neighbours into theirs. Try to sit upright with your hands either in your lap or resting lightly on the table. Don't put your elbows on the table: you might tip the table and you will make it difficult for those on either side of you to talk to each other.

If you are provided with a napkin, you should unfold it and lay it on your lap soon after sitting down. Napkins are not bibs; they are used to dab the mouth or chin for stray morsels.

Refusing things

If there are certain things you cannot eat, for whatever reason, try to warn your host when you reply to their invitation. If this is not possible, take only a small amount of the food and a large portion of accompanying foods, and then leave the 'offending' food as discreetly as possible. It is perfectly acceptable to refuse wine or any other kind of drink. To reinforce your refusal, lay your hand briefly over your glass.

Starting a meal

Should the host encourage you to start eating as soon as you are served, wait until one or two other people are ready to start eating and start at the same time as them. If you are unsure which cutlery to use or how to go about eating a particular kind of food, either ask or observe the tactics of more experienced diners. As a general rule, cutlery is laid in the correct order for the courses, with cutlery for the first course to the outside of each place setting.

There may be a small knife to the far right hand side of the place setting, this is for buttering bread. Butter should be taken from the butter dish using the butter knife provided, not your own knife. Bread rolls should be broken open and buttered a bit at a time.

Extras on the table

If there is something, such as an accompanying sauce, that you would like but cannot reach, either ask for it directly or offer it to your neighbour, hoping that they will eventually offer it to you. It is impolite to add salt and pepper to food without tasting it first; it implies you think the food will be bland.

All condiments and pickles should be put on the side of the plate and added to individual forkfuls of food; only Parmesan cheese, freshly ground pepper or salt from a salt mill are sprinkled directly over the food. You should not ask for things that are not on the table; this looks like a criticism of your host, and it would be doubly embarrassing if they did not have what you asked for. It is, however, acceptable to ask for a glass of water.

BASIC RULES

Coping with cutlery

The recognized way to hold cutlery is intended to make eating easy for you, and to stop you prodding your neighbour with your elbows. The most common cutlery combination is the knife and fork: the handle of the knife should nestle in the right hand with the first finger pointing along the top of the handle towards the blade; the thumb and second finger clamp the handle in place. The knife should only be used for cutting food and for pushing it onto the downturned prongs of the fork. It should not be used for shovelling food, and should never be brought to the mouth.

The fork should be held similarly: the handle nestling in the left hand, the first finger pointing along to the root of the tines, and the thumb and second finger clamping it in place. The tines should point downwards onto the plate and should prong the food so that it does not fall off on its way to the mouth. The fork should not really be used as a 'shovel' – although this is generally considered acceptable for rice and peas (see below) – and it should not be turned over in the right hand and used to cut food. Spaghetti and tagliatelle should be wound onto a fork in the bowl of a spoon. In the US, it is customary for the fork to be held in the right hand. Although this is becoming more acceptable it is really only suitable for less-formal occasions.

A soup spoon is held across the body, the end of its handle held down onto the first two fingers by the flat of the thumb. The spoon should be pushed away from the body not towards it, and brought to the mouth but not put in it. The soup should be poured from the side of the spoon into the mouth, not sucked. As you finish your soup, tip the bowl away from the body, not towards it, to spoon up the last of the soup.

If you have a spoon and fork for dessert, you should use both, manoeuvering food onto the spoon with the fork, which is held in the left hand. It is acceptable to use the fork alone, but not the spoon alone. Desserts served in small dishes or glasses are usually eaten with a teaspoon.

Cutlery should be lifted to the mouth, not the mouth lowered to the plate, and cutlery should never be waved about or used to emphasize a point in conversation. If you pause while you are eating, rest the cutlery on the plate, not the table; and at the end of each course put your cutlery down in a straight line up the centre of the plate.

Eating difficult foods

Certain foods are difficult to cope with, some are eaten with the fingers and others require special 'tools'. Foods such as peas and rice are very difficult to manage with a downturned fork, but at formal occasions this is the correct way of eating them, so cope as best you can. However, at a more relaxed, informal meal it is quite acceptable to turn the fork over and scoop the food up that way.

Foods eaten with the fingers that you are most likely to encounter include artichokes, asparagus and unpeeled prawns. When eating with your fingers never lick them, they should be wiped clean on a napkin and use a finger bowl if provided.

To eat an artichoke, remove each leaf individually, holding it by the fibrous tip dip the fleshy, white base in the sauce and then scrape the flesh off with your teeth. Discarded leaves should be arranged neatly on the edge of your plate, or separate dish if provided. The fluffy choke should not be eaten and the remaining heart is eaten with a knife and fork.

Whole asparagus, served as a separate dish, is eaten with the fingers. Pick each stalk up individually by the tougher, blunt end of the stem, and dip the pointed end in the accompanying sauce. The entire stalk may be eaten if the asparagus is young and tender, but if the end is tough just leave it on the side of your plate. Asparagus served as part of another dish should be eaten with a knife and fork.

When served unpeeled prawns, first pull off the tail, then ease the fleshy body away from the legs and shell, and finally tug it away from the head. If a sauce is provided dip it in it and then eat.

Many creatures served still in their shells are eaten with special 'tools'. For example, snails should be eaten with a special pair of tongs, which hold the shell steady, and a little pick or two-tined fork for prying the flesh from the shell. Fresh oysters in their shells should be eaten with a small fork. Use the fork in your right hand and hold the shell down with your left, and work the flesh free, then either lift the flesh out with the fork or tip the shell up and empty it straight into your mouth. Mussels may be served with a special pick for plucking out the flesh, or the flesh may be removed using another shell as a pincer. If lobster is served freshly cooked in its shell, scoop the flesh out with your knife and fork, and then cut it up as you would any other food. A special pick should be provided to extract the flesh from the claws.

Earning your meal

You can be considered to have earned your meal if you are courteous and considerate at table. Look after your neighbours and make sure that they have everything they need. Contribute to the conversation but don't dominate it, and compliment the host on the food.

Eat with your mouth shut and certainly don't speak with a mouthful, however eager you may be to make a point. Many people inadvertently say 'don't eat with your mouth full', when telling children not to speak with a mouthful. This slip of the tongue is in itself a sound piece of advice: eat only small mouthfuls – if your mouth is really full it will be difficult to keep it shut as you chew.

If you have to spit out any pips or chewy mouthfuls, do it as discreetly as possible. Pop them onto your fork and leave them on the side of the plate. If you spill a small amount of food or drink, ignore it; if you spill enough to cause possible damage, apologize and offer to help clear up or even pay for cleaning bills. Make as little fuss as possible and get back to your meal quickly.

Try to moderate the speed at which you eat so that you are neither waiting for ages with an empty plate nor keeping everyone else waiting. This is especially true if people have been asked to start eating before everyone is served. Keep an eye on the other plates around the table, to gauge your speed. Finally, however much you have enjoyed your food, don't doggedly scrape your plate clean; this is not only greedy, it also makes a lot of noise and can even damage the cutlery or the plate.

TABLE MANNERS – CHECKLIST

Important dos and don'ts

✔ **DO compliment the host on the food**
✔ **DO make sure you talk to both your neighbours**
✔ **DO ask for something (such as the salt), and never stretch across the table for it**
✗ **DON'T speak with your mouth full**
✗ **DON'T use our cutlery to emphasize your conversation**
✗ **DON'T lick your fingers**

BASIC RULES

What not to do

You should not scratch or sniff at table. If you have to cough or sneeze, turn away from the table and cover your face with a hand or handkerchief. In general, you should try not to leave the table during a meal, but if you choke you may have to: do so quietly and return quickly. Don't eat with your fingers unless the host does, and never lick your fingers. If a dish – such as artichokes – requires you to use your fingers, finger bowls should be provided: dip your fingers in the water and dry them on your napkin.

If you see someone coming round with the wine bottle, don't automatically drain your glass to make room for as much wine as possible. Finally, many people find smoking completely incompatible with eating: don't smoke without asking, and try not to even ask until the meal is over.

TELEPHONE ETIQUETTE

The telephone is the most important and efficient form of communication in use today. Whether at home or at work, we should all spare a little thought for the way in which we use it.

A telephone manner

When using the telephone it is important to remember that you only have your voice with which to communicate. Without the added help of persuasive eye contact and expressive hand movements your voice may seem abrupt, bored or stiffly formal. To avoid this you should speak clearly, concisely and as naturally as possible; and you should be especially polite.

If you have to spell something out on the telephone, use words to distinguish between letters that sound very much the same: for example 'F for Freddy' and 'S for sugar'.

By the law of averages, some telephone conversations will turn into arguments. If you are arguing with someone on the telephone, try to keep calm, and express your point of view succinctly and calmly. Allow the other person time to express his or her ideas without interruption. Never slam the receiver down on someone who annoys you on the telephone; this is not only very rude, it is actually a sign of weakness or defeat. If you do cut a telephone call off, you should ring back immediately to apologize.

Making calls

Before making a call, consider whether or not it is a suitable time. It is unfair to make a complicated business call in the last few minutes before someone is due to leave the office. Private calls – unless they are to close family – should be made after

10 am and before 10 pm. You should avoid making telephone calls from someone else's house, but if you have to you should offer to pay for the call.

If you dial a wrong number, do not simply hang up – this can be alarming for the person answering the telephone: apologize first.

When you get through to someone, be polite to whoever answers the telephone, and state clearly who you are and who you would like to speak to. If you call an office and are put through to someone you do not know, ask for his or her name, so that – if necessary – you can refer to your conversation with him or her in the future.

Ask the person you have called whether it is a good time to call, and if not arrange another time. Whether the call concerns business or your personal life, be prepared: have ready any relevant information and a pen and paper (see below). If you make or confirm an arrangement, make a note of it immediately, and preferably write to confirm it.

The telephone is a useful way of keeping in touch with friends, but sometimes it offers a lazy option. For example, thank-yous and replies to formal invitations should be made in writing. You can use the telephone to accept an invitation only if the telephone number is given with the letters RSVP on the invitation. At work, you should make and accept a minimum of personal calls.

Answering calls

When you answer a telephone call give your number or, at work, the name of the company. Women, especially those who live alone, are advised not to give their names when answering the telephone, in case the caller becomes a nuisance. If you have been called at a very inconvenient time, let the caller know and arrange a better time when you can ring them back. If they ask to speak to someone else, don't set about finding the other person or connecting the call without letting the caller know you are doing so.

Messages

It can be very frustrating to receive incomplete written messages or half-remembered verbal ones. Telephone messages should always be written down straight away, and should include the date and time of the call, the caller's name (and the name of the company for a business call) and telephone number, the reason they called and whether or not they will ring back or would like to be contacted.

TELEPHONE ETIQUETTE – CHECKLIST

Important dos and don'ts

✓ **DO check that it's a good time to call**
✓ **DO be specially polite on the telephone**
✓ **DO take detailed messages**
✗ **DON'T keep people holding without letting them know why**
✗ **DON'T hang up half way through a conversation**
✗ **DON'T telephone early in the morning or late at night**

Answering machines

Although many people are a little frightened of leaving messages on answering machines, these devices are useful for keeping in touch with those who are rarely at home. If someone has gone to the trouble of buying an answering machine, the least a caller can do is to leave a message on it.

The outgoing message on the machine should let the caller know when to speak and – to some extent – what to say; it may also tell them how long they have for their message. With most machines, the caller is asked to speak after the tone or series of tones. They should give the date and time of their call, their name and telephone number, and the reason they called. When the messages are played back, they should be responded to promptly.

TIPPING

Many people are unsure when, who and how much to tip. The important thing to remember about tipping is that it is entirely at your discretion, so have the courage of your convictions. Tipping originated as a way of rewarding good work, particularly of those on low wages such as waiting staff. Many hotels and restaurants now add a service charge, so you need only tip if the staff were especially helpful.

Waiters, hotel staff, taxi drivers and hairdressers commonly receive tips amounting to 10% (or 15%) of the bill, especially if they have been pleasant and helpful or have worked late for the customer. If possible, leave a tip in cash so that the individual concerned has a greater chance of receiving it directly. It is inappropriate to tip professional people, such as nurses or solicitors, or the proprietors of hotels, restaurants and hairdressing salons.

CHRISTENINGS

A christening is essentially a religious ceremony during which an individual – usually a baby – is first embraced as a member of the Christian faith. It is not a legal procedure, nor is it compulsory.

When and where

There is no set age at which a baby is expected to be christened, in fact some people are not christened or baptized until adulthood. However, christenings usually happen when the baby is about six weeks old – when the parents have had a chance to establish some sort of routine in the newborn's life.

The christening ceremony usually takes place in the parents' local parish church or a church that they attend regularly. In any event, the parents have to ask the incumbent vicar for permission for their child to be christened in his church. If for any reason they would like the ceremony to be held in another church, they again have to seek the permission of that church's vicar.

It is often the case that, if the parents are not churchgoers, they will be dissuaded by the priest or vicar from having their child christened, unless they intend to go to church in the future. The parents should then think carefully about just why they wish their child to be christened.

The ceremony

The child's parents should discuss the service with their local vicar or priest, who will explain how he likes to conduct christenings. The parents may want the ceremony to be held in the church privately. However, the Church of England prefers to conduct a baptism during the Sunday service. The parents may wish to invite another vicar to officiate at the ceremony; and should introduce this idea tactfully to the incumbent vicar, who technically has the right to say no.

There may or may not be a small charge for the christening service; if not – or if the charge is very small – the parents should show their gratitude by making a donation to the church fund.

Christenings are usually fairly small gatherings, and guests can be invited by telephone or by written invitation. As with other religious ceremonies, dress should be fairly formal. During the ceremony, those immediately involved in the christening should gather around the font; other guests and well-wishers should choose pews nearest the font.

Not every family has a suitable christening gown handed down through the generations. This is not a prerequisite of christenings, in fact it is perhaps more practical to clothe the baby in a simple, smart outfit in traditional white. Babies can not be expected to understand and respect the formality of a church service. If your baby screams during his or her christening, don't panic; no-one should mind and the more tense you are the more inclined the baby will be to carry on crying.

Godparents

Most denominations require godparents to sponsor a child at his or her christening. In the Church of England service there are traditionally two godparents of the same sex of the child and one of the opposite sex, although there may be more. The Church of Scotland requires no godparents. When a mature person is baptized he or she chooses two sponsors.

Godparents are primarily intended to ensure that their godchild is brought up in the Christian faith. Most vicars, therefore, insist that godparents have themselves been baptized and, preferably, confirmed in the Christian Church. During the service the godparents are asked to affirm their faith and to vow that they will see that the child is brought up in that faith; at some time during the ceremony, they may each hold the baby.

Although less importance is now attached to the religious role of the godparent, being a godparent is still a responsibility that should be taken seriously. Godparents should show an interest in the child's growth and upbringing. Ideally, they should be close and trustworthy friends of the family and, therefore, see the child regularly. They should make a point of remembering birthdays and Christmas. Parents should bear all this in mind when choosing godparents. When you ask friends to be god-parents for your children, you should write to them. This allows them an opportunity to think about your proposal, and makes it easier for them to decline, should they want to.

If you are invited to be a godparent, you may be very flattered, but you should give some thought to the invitation before accepting it. If you feel that you are inadequate as a religious sponsor or if you know you do not have time to be a good god-parent, it is fairer to decline tactfully – giving your reasons – than to accept and be a disappointment. If you would like to be the child's godparent, but cannot attend the christening ceremony you can be represented by a proxy on the day.

After the ceremony

It is usual for the parents to hold a small informal reception after a christening ceremony. Depending on the time of day, this may be a quick drink, afternoon tea or a full meal. The vicar or priest should always be invited to this reception and, if a meal is eaten, he should be asked to say grace.

At some stage during the reception, one of the godparents should propose a toast to the baby's future. This toast may be drunk in champagne, although wine or even tea are equally acceptable. There is usually a christening cake: a rich, iced, fruit cake (some parents carry on the tradition of saving the top tier of their wedding cake as a christening cake – but only for the first child!).

Christening presents

Godparents and close family members usually give christening presents that have lasting value: a piece of silver or jewellery, premium bonds or even a savings account opened in the child's name. Other guests are not expected to bring presents and certainly not valuable ones. If they choose to bring something to celebrate the christening, something more immediately useful – such as clothes or a toy – would be appropriate.

CHRISTMAS CARDS AND PRESENTS

Many companies as well as individuals like to send out Christmas cards; some may even have cards specially printed with their name and address. Whether or not the cards are printed, they should all be signed by hand.

Guidelines for cards

Some people like to send a card to virtually everyone they know, including those they see every day at work. Others prefer to send cards only to those they see rarely, and they may include a letter with the card. It is entirely up to you to decide whether or not you want to send Christmas cards, and who you would like to send them to. In general you should stick to your list even if you receive unexpected cards from people you didn't send cards to yourself. If, however, someone continues to send you a card every year, it would only be fair to add them to your list.

Guidelines for presents

Christmas presents are usually given only to family and close friends. Different families attach more or less importance to Christmas presents, and spend corresponding amounts of money on them. If you are newly married, check with your spouse how his or her family deals with Christmas presents. It may be the custom for some people to make lists of things they would like, others prefer being given surprises; some people prefer to give one present to each family group, others like to give a little something to each person.

Similarly, when you spend your first Christmas in a new job, ask someone what the company policy is on Christmas presents. It would be embarrassing not to reciprocate if your colleagues all gave you little presents.

DINNER PARTIES

Dinner parties are a very popular form of entertaining. Whatever the choice of menu, number of people and degree of formality, a dinner party gives you an opportunity to offer your friends hospitality and to introduce them to each other.

Advance planning

Once you have decided to hold a dinner party you should begin planning about three weeks in advance. Before inviting too many people, check how many you can seat comfortably round your table or tables, and make sure that you have enough matching crockery and cutlery for them.

You should also check that your finances and your culinary skills can cope with the numbers. Be sure that the meal does not comprise too many elements that require your attention at the last minute – especially if you are a solo host. Otherwise you may find that you are forced to abandon your guests too much before and during the meal, spending most of your time in the kitchen or carrying things to and from it.

Plan your combination of guests so that each of them has something in common with at least one other person, and avoid bringing together individuals who are bound to disagree heatedly on any subject. Keep a note of who comes to your dinner parties and what you gave them for dinner, then you can avoid asking the same combinations of friends again or serving people the same dish twice.

Invitations

Guests can be invited to dinner parties by telephone or by written invitation. Written invitations should go out a good three weeks before the chosen date. Telephone invitations should be made about ten days in advance. Once a telephone invitation has been accepted some hosts like to send an 'at home' card with the letters RSVP crossed out and replaced with the letters PM (from the French Pour Mémoireé – as a reminder).

An invitation should indicate the date, time and place of the dinner; it should also give guests some idea of what to wear, and it may let them know that the evening has been planned to celebrate something. Written invitations should also give an address or telephone number for replies.

If you can only fit eight people round your table, ask only eight people. If someone says that they are unable to come you still have time to invite someone else; but if you invite more people in the first place and they all accept you will have logistical problems. When you invite a single person, check whether there is someone he or she would particularly like to bring. Don't worry if the final guest list has more of one sex than another, and don't shy away from mixing different age groups.

As with any invitation, guests should reply to dinner party invitations as soon as possible. This is especially true if you can not attend. The more swiftly you decline an invitation, the more time it gives your hosts to fill the gap. If you are a vegetarian or have any food allergies you should let your hosts know when you reply to the invitation. Even if they ask you fairly often, it is safest to remind them of these preferences every time they invite you.

Laying the table
The table should be laid in advance so that hosts are free to greet guests and keep an eye on the kitchen. The way that you lay the table for a dinner party is governed partly by convention and

partly by personal choice. You may choose to use a tablecloth to hide a cluster of mismatched little tables or to protect a valuable wooden surface, or you may prefer to show off your table and use place mats only.

Each place setting should have the cutlery – with forks on the left, and knives and spoons on the right – in the correct order for the courses, with the cutlery for the first course on the outside. Knives should be laid with the blade facing inwards, and forks with the tines facing upwards. If you are short of space small knives may be put on the side plate (to the left of the place setting) and dessert spoons and forks can be put above the place setting: the fork nearest the place setting with tines to the right-hand side, and the spoon above it with the bowl to the left-hand side.

Glasses are laid just above the knives. There should be a different glass for each wine to be served, and a separate glass for water. If you are simply offering a choice of red or white wine, each guest will probably only need one glass, but you should have spare glasses available in case they want to change wines with the different courses. Special glasses should be brought to the table at the appropriate time for port, brandy or liqueurs.

Napkins may be folded simply or ornately and laid on the place setting or the side plate. Salad plates, if used, should be laid just above the place setting to the left-hand side. If you have little holders for name cards, these should be placed directly above the place setting. Salts, peppers and sauce boats should be dotted in groups evenly around the table.

It may be easier to have the first course ready and laid at each place setting in advance (although this is, of course, not practical with a hot first course). Some hosts like to lay the dinner plate underneath the first course to show off their dinner service. Others prefer to warm the dinner plates or to keep them on the sideboard from which the main course will be served.

SPECIAL OCCASIONS

Arriving on time

Most people realize that the arrival time stated on an invitation does not need to be observed with military precision, but the leeway around that time depends on the sort of function and on how well you know the host.

Unless you know your host very well – and can help with the last-minute panic – it is unfair to arrive before the stated time. It is better to drive around for ten minutes or even to stop and have a drink nearby, than to arrive ahead of time. Most hosts actually expect people to arrive a little late and you may catch them out even if you arrive at the appointed time.

In general, the first guests arrive within 10 or 15 minutes of the stated time, and everyone should be there within half an hour of it. In busy and congested cities late arrivals seem to be more acceptable than in the country. Acceptability also depends on the size of the gathering: if you arrive very late you should cause little trouble at a large buffet dinner, but you could ruin or at least seriously disrupt a smaller sit-down meal. If you know that you are going to be late, telephone your host

If, when you receive the invitation, you know that your commitments on that day are bound to make you late, let your host know in your reply, and tell them that you will quite understand if they would rather you did not come at all. If on the day itself you are held up by unforeseen circumstances, try to call your host to reassure them that you are on your way, give some indication of when you think you will arrive, and urge them to start eating without you if this seems appropriate.

You should be especially attentive to punctuality if the invitation says 7.30 for 8.00. This implies that you will actually be sitting down to eat at 8 o'clock, and you should, therefore, arrive not later than 7.50. If you have been invited to a surprise dinner party, you should aim to be extremely punctual so that you are in place ready for the surprise and don't give the game away by bumping into the 'surprisee' in the hall!

Bringing a gift

Some guests like to bring a gift when they arrive at a dinner party, and bring-a-bottle parties have popularized the idea of bringing a bottle of wine. Wine is not, however, always a good choice, because the host has usually bought wine to go with the meal. It would be embarrassing if you brought a cheaper wine or embarrassing for the host if you brought a better one. In any event, do not expect your wine to be served during the meal.

A box of chocolates or other confectionery, a bunch of flowers or a small pot plant are good alternatives. If the dinner party has been arranged to celebrate a birthday, engagement, promotion, house-warming or some other event, a bottle of champagne or a gift appropriate to the occasion would be well received.

Receiving guests

Hosts should make a point of greeting each guest at the door, rather than hoping that another guest will helpfully answer the door bell. Depending on the time of year and the weather, you must be prepared for the fact that guests may arrive with coats and/or umbrellas; work out in advance where they can put these, instead of dumping them unceremoniously as people arrive.

When guests arrive, the first priority is to offer them a drink. It is up to you to decide what you would like to give them: you may offer the full gamut of spirits, or a choice of red or white wine, or one specific cocktail, such as Pimms, that you have made for the occasion. Whatever you decide, soft drinks should always be available as an alternative.

You may also serve canapés or just crisps and nuts before the meal. These are particularly useful if everyone is getting hungry waiting for a late guest or a last minute hold-up in the kitchen. It

SPECIAL OCCASIONS

is not worth making nibbles too complicated though, and it is a shame to make them so filling or so spicy that they detract from the meal itself.

If you are hosting a dinner party alone, you may decide to elect one of your guests to help with serving the drinks, then you will be free to introduce newcomers while someone else gets them a drink. Only introduce people a few at a time, and give them some information about each other to help them start a conversation. If someone brings an uninvited guest with them, you have to bite your tongue and welcome them, whatever logistical nightmares this implies at the table and in the kitchen.

Seating your guests

When the meal is ready, the host or hostess will let his or her guests know that it is time to sit down. Guests should then move directly to the table and not go rushing off to the toilet or launching into a long anecdote, which may endanger a carefully timed soufflé. Women should lead the way to the table and should sit first. They should hesitate before sitting to check whether the hosts are likely to want to say grace.

Seating plans should be made in advance. For a large dinner, it may be helpful for the host to have a little diagram of the seating arrangements for guests to check before sitting down to dinner. The rules governing seating plans are no longer as rigid as they once were. It is easiest for hosts to choose a person or couple that they consider to be guest or guests of honour; these people should be seated to the right of the host and/or hostess. with this starting point, the other guests can be arranged, ideally alternating men and women, round the table. Most people like to split up couples at the dinner table, but it should be remembered that it is traditional for engaged and newly-married couples to stay together.

If you have invited more than eight people, the course of the conversation will tend to break up into splinter groups. You should, therefore, plan your seating so that each guest is next to or opposite someone who shares his or her interests.

The courses

The number of courses that you choose to serve depends largely on your powers of organization and your supplies of crockery. Most dinner parties include a first course, a main course, dessert and cheese. The cheese may be served before the dessert. There is of course nothing wrong with serving only three of these four courses. Similarly, you may choose to include more courses: for example a fish and/or sorbet course may be served between the first and main courses, you may serve a savoury after the dessert, and fruit after the cheese.

Serving the meal

If you are hosting a party alone, it would be a good idea to put one of your guests in charge of the wine so that they can keep people's glasses topped up while you serve the food. You may decide to leave the wine on the table for guests to help themselves. You should still keep an eye on glasses to make sure that everyone is getting enough to drink. Wine glasses should not be filled more than two-thirds full. Water should also be available.

If your dining room is large enough, you may decide to invite guests to get up between courses and serve themselves to food from a sideboard. It is, however, more traditional to serve the guests. You may give them empty plates and then come round the table with each dish so that they can help themselves. In this case you should always serve from the left-hand side (if you happen to know that a guest is left-handed, serve them from the right, which he or she will find easier). Sometimes it is more practical to pass serving dishes around, or to put some or all of them on the table for guests to help themselves.

During the meal

Guests should start to eat when the hostess does, or when she urges them to if the serving is taking some time. Before starting to eat, they should ensure that those on either side of them have everything they need.

The hosts are responsible for ensuring that the conversation flows, and that all the guests are given an opportunity to contribute to it. They must diffuse heated discussions and fill awkward pauses. They should also make sure that the meal progresses at a reasonable speed, not rushing the courses so that people's plates are whisked away before they have put their cutlery down, but not dawdling so that guests are longing to get home before the dessert has been served.

When clearing courses the hosts should not stack the plates noisily or messily scrape the remains of food from one plate to another at the table. All salts, peppers and sauces should be cleared after the main course. If guests offer to help with the clearing – or with any part of the administration of the meal – these offers should be genuine and not merely token gestures. Some hosts will eagerly accept offers of help, but others would rather manage on their own, and may hate it if other people 'trespass' into their kitchen. If other guests are helping, don't feel you have to leap up and join in. Stay sitting and keep the conversation going, and then offer to help with the next course. If your hosts have said they don't want any help, it is not fair to ignore their wishes, however much you think they might value your help.

If port is served – usually with the cheese course – it should be given first to the person to the right-hand side of the host, then passed to the left, clockwise round the table. Even if you are not drinking port, don't ignore the decanter, and make sure that you pass it on.

Coffee and liqueurs may be served at the table or elsewhere, although moving the guests may interrupt the flow of conversation. In some households the hostess and other ladies follow the tradition of withdrawing after the meal to 'powder their noses', leaving the men to linger over drinks at the table. This apparently old-fashioned idea is actually a practical way of ensuring that only half the guest are trying to use the bathroom at any one time. The ladies then have coffee in the sitting room where they are joined by the men. No-one should begin smoking until after the meal is finished. (See also **Table Manners** in the Basic Rules section.)

Leaving

The time to leave a dinner party is often dictated by the pace of the meal itself. If you know that you are going to have to leave in good time, warn your host beforehand and leave as discreetly as possible so as not to break up the evening. If the meal goes on a long time and you very much want to leave, you should really stay until coffee is offered, decline it politely and then leave.

During the week, most people have to think about getting to work the next day and leave at a reasonable time. Weekend dinner parties may go on until the early hours of the morning. Whatever the circumstances and however much you are enjoying yourself, make sure that you are not keeping your hosts up. If in doubt, say 'I must be going'; they will be quick to protest if they would like you to stay on.

Hosts can find a number of ways of letting guests know that they feel the evening has come to an end. If they get frantic they can offer to call for a taxi or even excuse themselves and slip off to bed! Ideally, they should make sure that all of their guests have their coats and they should see each of them to the door.

SPECIAL OCCASIONS

Thanking

Guests should not leave a dinner party without saying goodbye to and thanking their hosts. They should also ring, or preferably write, soon after the dinner to thank their hosts for the evening.

DINNER PARTIES – CHECKLIST

Important dos and don'ts

✓ **DO plan a big party at least three weeks in advance**

✓ **DO arrive in good time; no more than half an hour late**

✓ **DO remember to thank your hosts, at the time and a day or so after**

✗ **DON'T invite too disparate a collection of people, but don't worry about balancing the sexes or mixing age groups**

✓ **DON'T outstay your welcome**

ENGAGEMENTS

An engagement is one of the most exciting events in a person's life. It is also a momentous one, heralding great changes. Couples are not, however, legally required to become engaged before getting married (see Weddings in this section).

Asking the question

The way in which couples become engaged varies a great deal, and may be governed by their financial means. Either partner may 'pop the question' and they may choose to do so at any time. Some men like to organize a lavish dinner or even a holiday as a setting for their proposal, others literally go down on bended knee, whereas some couples will just agree 'well, let's get married then' halfway through an apparently ordinary conversation.

It is no longer considered necessary for the man to ask his prospective father-in-law in advance for his daughter's hand in marriage, but the bride's parents should be the first to know, especially as they traditionally pay for the wedding.

The ring need not be produced at once and, in fact, many couples like to choose the ring together, finding a compromise between their tastes and their budget. The ring may be an antique, it may be bought new, made specially or it may even be a family heirloom. It may have any combination of stones, although diamonds or diamonds mixed with other stones are the most enduringly popular.

Some couples talk of 'getting engaged' when they mean formally announcing their engagement. Once two people have agreed that they will eventually marry they are engaged, whether or not they choose to make the fact public.

SPECIAL OCCASIONS

If a proposal thrills you, but takes you completely by surprise it is perfectly acceptable to ask for time to consider. It is far better to take a little time at this stage than to make a terrible mistake or to pass up on the opportunity of a lifetime.

Refusing

If someone asks you to marry them and you do not want to accept their proposal, you should deal with the question as tactfully and delicately as possible. A proposal of marriage is probably the most difficult offer anyone ever makes to another person. They have considered it carefully and are putting a great deal on the line. If you really do not want to accept it is best to say so straight away, rather than to ask for time to think and keep the other person in suspense. Tell them that you are very flattered by their proposal but that you can not accept it, and try – as gently as possible – to give them your reasons.

Announcing an engagement

The bride's parents should be the first to hear the happy news, swiftly followed by the groom's parents and any other close family or friends who should be informed in person, by telephone or letter. Should both or either of the partners be widowed or divorced they should also let their former parents-in-law know of their new engagement. This is especially true if they have children who remain in close contact with their in-laws.

It is not essential to run to the expense of a newspaper announcement – whether local or national – though many couples like to. Scan through other announcements in the newspaper of your choice to work out the format for the wording. The cost of newspaper announcements is traditionally borne by the bride's parents. If you expect them to pay, you should check that they are in agreement before booking the space.

Once an engagement is made public, the couple may receive a great many cards, letters and even small engagement presents. If you want to congratulate a newly-engaged couple, you should offer the man congratulations and the woman your best wishes. The couple should write and thank all their well-wishers as promptly as possible.

Engagement parties

There is no need to have a formal engagement party, although some couples choose to have a large gathering so that all their friends can meet and at which they can formally announce their engagement. The North American custom of holding 'shower parties' is beginning to take on in the UK. Friends are invited to a 'paper shower' or a 'glass shower', for example, and each guest brings an appropriate gift, for instance some writing paper or a glass bowl.

If the parents of the prospective bride and groom have not yet met, a meeting should be arranged as soon as possible after the engagement. Traditionally, the groom's parents invite the bride's parents for a meal. At any such meal or engagement party, speeches are not necessary, but a toast should be proposed to the engaged couple.

During the engagement

The main function of an engagement is to prepare – both emotionally and practically – for the wedding. The length of an engagement may be dictated by how long it is likely to take to organize the wedding. A register office ceremony takes little time to arrange, but it is generally considered that a full church wedding with a large reception can not be satisfactorily organized in much less than three months. There may be many other factors governing the length of an engagement, for example one of the partners may be waiting to start a particular job, or one of them may be waiting to finish his or her studies. There is no rule for how long an engagement should last.

The engaged couple may decide to have engagement photographs taken. These may be expensive, but they are often worthwhile because they are taken at leisure, usually in a studio, and may, therefore, be more flattering than wedding photographs.

The future bride and groom should always be invited to functions together. If either partner is invited to something on their own, he or she may ring the hosts to let them know of the engagement and to ask whether his or her partner is also invited. Traditionally, engaged couples are not split up in seating plans for sit-down lunches and dinners. However, they should not be too demonstrative about their affection for each other in public: a little affection is endearing, too much is embarrassing.

Breaking off engagements

The breaking off of an engagement is a very painful and difficult thing to do. If, however, you feel that, for whatever reason, you can not go through with a marriage, you should discuss it with your partner as soon as possible. Although it is unpleasant to break off an engagement, the unhappiness caused by a broken engagement can not compare with the anguish and expense of a failed marriage.

When a couple break off their engagement the woman should return her engagement ring, and both partners should return any valuable gifts they have received from each other, especially family heirlooms. They should let their families and close friends know as soon as possible, but should keep the painful reasons to themselves. Others should respect their privacy and should not talk about the break up, helping the partners to start their lives again. If a newspaper announcement was made at the time of the engagement, the couple may wish to put a simple announcement in the same newspaper to say that their wedding will now not be taking place.

If the engagement had progressed to the stage where wedding invitations had been sent out, the wedding hosts (usually the bride's parents) should write or send a typed note to all the guests, explaining that the wedding will not take place. If any wedding presents had already been received, they should be returned with a brief letter of gratitude and explanation.

ENGAGEMENTS – CHECKLIST

Important dos and don'ts

√ **DO tell both sets of parents as soon as possible**
√ **DO agree for an engagement of several months if a large wedding has to be planned**
X **DON'T refuse without consideration for the proposer**

ETIQUETTE ABROAD

It is virtually impossible to generalize about etiquette in other countries because traditions and courtesies vary so much from one country to another, even from one region to another. It is, however, true to say that basic good manners speak most languages. The best way to tackle the problem of etiquette abroad is to have the correct attitude to your host nation: be tolerant, adapt quickly and always show respect.

What to wear

Some nations may appear to attach more importance than the British to punctuality and formality, and you should respect this. Always pay attention to notices about dress codes. For example, on beaches some countries do not tolerate nudity or topless sunbathing, while others cannot accept bare arms in public. Many prefer people to be well covered up when entering places of worship. It is best to arrive at any function covered up and what may appear to you to be overdressed – you can always remove layers of clothing and of formality. If you have any doubt about what is expected, it is always better to ask rather than give offence inadvertently.

Communicating

It is polite to attempt to speak to waiters and shop assistants in their own language, rather than assuming that they speak English. If they do, they will soon put you out of your misery. Take a small dictionary or phrase book with you to help make yourself understood. If you go to someone's home or travel in remote regions, your company will be much more welcome if you show a willingness to speak the host language. Any attempt at communication is usually appreciated, for example, it is polite to ask before taking a photograph of someone, instead of treating them like an inanimate tourist attraction or part of the scenery.

The pitfalls of tipping

Tipping may cause problems abroad. In some countries a service charge is automatically added to bills, so you should check bills before parting with a tip unnecessarily. If in doubt give a small tip. In some instances you will be left in no doubt that a tip is expected, for example in many other European countries cinema usherettes will hover around after showing you to your seat, waiting for you to hand them a small tip.

ETIQUETTE ABROAD – CHECKLIST

Important dos and don'ts

✓ **DO find out about a country's customs**
✓ **DO make an effort to speak the language**
✗ **DON'T be afraid to ask, it won't give offence and shows consideration**
✗ **DON'T assume that being British is good manners enough**

Check before you go

If you are going to spend any length of time in a country or are going on a business trip there, it is best to read about the country beforehand or even to contact the embassy to ask for guidance. You need to know, for example, that in France you should always say 'bonjour, madame/monsieur' and 'au revoir, madame/monsieur' when entering and leaving a shop. In many countries you should send flowers to a hostess after a party. In African countries the elderly are treated with special respect, while in Japan it is a great honour to be invited to someone's home. There are countless other examples of points of etiquette that are peculiar to one or a few countries. You can only hope to discover them by reading about the country concerned and going there with an open mind.

FORMAL AND ROYAL OCCASIONS

Every once in a while you may be invited to a very formal function, such as a military ceremony, a Lord Mayor's dinner or even a royal garden party. You may have no idea how to respond to the invitation, what to wear, when to arrive, how to behave and when to leave. If you observe a few golden rules, you should be able to enjoy even the most formal of occasions.

General guidelines

Try not to be too nervous about special functions; you won't enjoy yourself if you are worrying the whole time. If possible check with the organization that invited you if you are unsure about any details. Arrive punctually and watch other people to check what they are doing. Stay standing if the guest of honour is standing, and finally, don't leave before the guest of honour does, but don't stay on long after he or she has left.

Formal invitations

Happily, invitations to formal functions often carry far more information than more everyday invitations, and this is certainly the case with royal functions. The wording will be formal, and you should reply promptly and in equally formal terms, referring to yourself in the third person, for example: 'Mr and Mrs Marcus Taylor thank General Sir John Vaughan for his kind invitation to . . . .'.

If the invitation does not indicate what you should wear, or if there is any other information you need before accepting, ring the organizers of the function (or the press office at Buckingham Palace, if it is a royal occasion) to check.

SPECIAL OCCASIONS

Royal invitations will usually tell you what to wear, when to arrive and even where to park. Invitations from the Queen or the Queen Mother are really commands and should only be refused in exceptional circumstances. Royal invitations will usually come from the private secretary of the relevant member of the royal family. You should send a handwritten reply to this personal secretary. Your reply should begin, for example, 'Miss Faith Buxton presents her compliments to the private secretary to the Prince of Wales...'. When you accept a royal invitation your reply should end, '... and has the honour to obey Her Majesty's [or Her/His Royal Highness's] command'. (See also **Letter Writing**: Replying to formal invitations; The Envelope – in the Basic Rules section.)

Introductions and meeting royalty

Always wait to be introduced to a guest of honour – royal or otherwise – rather than introducing yourself.

If you meet a member of the royal family in an informal setting, such as a walkabout, you may feel overawed. If you are not sure what to do or say, try not to worry: most members of the royal family are used to dealing with the general public. If you are invited to a royal function, you will usually be warned if you are to be introduced to a member of the royal family, and you will be told how to address him or her.

The Queen and the Queen Mother should be addressed initially as Your Majesty; all other royals are Your Royal Highness or Your Highness. In subsequent conversation, they are called sir or ma'am (pronounced like ham not harm). If you are introduced to royalty, you should not offer your hand to be shaken, but you should respond rapidly if the royal personage offers his or hers. Men should bow their heads as they are introduced, and ladies should curtsy. If you are not confident about curtsying, practise at home: Put the toes of one foot down just behind the heel of the other foot, and bend your knees, keeping you back and head upright, but lowering your eyes.

It is now considered acceptable for commoners to instigate conversation with royals, although they should avoid contentious topics and should not ask personal questions. While talking to a member of the royal family you should not use the words 'you' and 'yours', but should substitute 'your Royal Highness' and 'your Royal Highness's'. If the conversation goes on for any length of time, however, you may feel you can relax a little and drop this very formal way of speaking.

See also **Introductions** in the Basic Rules section, and **Forms of Address** at the end of the book.

Inviting royalty

If you are organizing a formal or charity function, you may want to invite a member of the royal family as guest of honour. You should first contact his or her private secretary by telephone, well in advance, to check whether he or she might be free and willing to attend the function. If this initial telephone invitation is successful, write to the private secretary to confirm the invitation and then write – via the private secretary – to officially invite the royal personage. You should not invite more than one member of the royal family to any one event. But if the person you contacted first is unable to attend, it is perfectly acceptable to go on and try to invite another member of the royal family.

Before the function itself, the private secretary will let you know when your royal guest will arrive; the secretary may also give you other information, for example he or she may advise you on what your royal guest does not like to eat if the function includes a meal. You will probably be asked about yourself and about any other people to whom the royal guest will be formally introduced.

SPECIAL OCCASIONS

When you send out printed invitations for the function to your other guests, the invitation should indicate the time at which your royal guest will be arriving, so that all the other guests can arrive before that time. If you introduce people to the royal guest, you should ask him or her: 'Your Royal Highness, may I introduce . . .'. After the function, you should write to the royal guest to thank him or her for attending.

Formal meals and toasts

If you are not sure of the sequence of events, keep an eye on other people. At some functions the guest of honour or all those seated at the High Table, may proceed to their places before the other guests; at others they may arrive when all the other guests are already standing behind their allotted seats, or when they are already seated. Sometimes the other guests are expected to clap as the guests of honour arrive.

Don't sit down without checking whether the moment to sit has come. You may have to wait until the guest of honour has been seated, grace has been said or the national anthem has been played. Hesitate also before you start eating or drinking, there may be some preamble you have not predicted. If there is a menu on the table, it is a good idea to have a look at it: it may give you a clue about the sequence of the meal and any toasts that may be drunk.

If port is served, make sure that you pass it on (always to the person on your left), especially if there are many toasts so that people's glasses may need topping up frequently. When you first fill your port glass, check before taking a sip from it; at many formal dinners the 'loyal toast' is said before the first sip of port is taken. One person will propose the loyal toast by standing and saying, 'Ladies and gentlemen, the Queen'. All the other guests will stand, holding their glasses, and say 'the Queen'. They then take a sip of their port before sitting down again. At naval functions it is customary to remain seated for the loyal toast.

If there are other toasts, guests may or may not be expected to remain seated: if you are not sure, check what those around you do. If you do not drink port, it is perfectly correct to drink a toast with a soft drink.

No-one should start smoking until after the toasts are over, unless the host has announced that people may smoke. When coffee is served, or when the ladies withdraw at the end of the meal, guests may begin smoking. No guest should leave the meal before the guest of honour has left. When the guest of honour leaves, the other guests usually get to their feet until he or she has left the room. They may then leave immediately or sit back down, although they are expected to leave shortly.

See also **Table Manners** in the Basic Rules section and **Dinner Parties** in this one.

Royal garden parties

If you are invited to a royal garden party and will be attending, you need not write to accept the invitation. If, however, you cannot attend you should write to say that you are unable to attend the garden party, and you should also return the 'admittance card' which will have been sent with the invitation. This admittance card is important: you should not lose it and should take it with you to the garden party as it acts as a pass to Buckingham Palace or Holyrood House, depending on where the garden party is being held.

The invitation will give you a good deal of information about the day, including where to park. Men are required to wear lounge suits or morning dress, or – if applicable – uniforms, national or clerical dress. Ladies should be dressed smartly, and many choose to wear a hat. It is wise to wear comfortable shoes as you will walk some distance and will spend several hours on your feet. You should also make sure that you are equipped with warm clothes and an umbrella if the weather threatens to be inclement.

You should not expect to be introduced to members of the royal family; only a small proportion of the hundreds of people present can hope to receive this honour. People will form lines, making a path for the royal party; it will be obvious if a member of the royal family is making their way towards you. If not, you should not push your way to a place where you are bound to be introduced to him or her.

The end of the garden party will be indicated by the playing of the National Anthem at 6.00 pm. The royal party will then leave, and all the guests are expected to leave shortly after this. (It is acceptable to leave a garden party before the royal party has left.) After attending a royal garden party, there is no obligation to write and thank the relevant member of the royal family, although there is nothing to stop you doing so.

Other royal functions

Members of the royal family may attend award ceremonies, investitures, charity balls and state banquets. Invitations to any of these occasions will tell you what to wear. Most evening functions will require white tie for men (or uniform or national dress) and long dress (or national dress) for women. Daytime functions usually require morning dress or lounge suits for men (or uniforms, national or clerical dress) and smart day wear for women. Many women like to wear hats for formal daytime functions, but they should bear in mind that large hats may obscure the view for other guests at religious and other ceremonies.

At royal and state banquets, guests should not take their seats until the royal party and guests of honour are seated. At the end of the meal, the National Anthem will be played and the royal party will then leave; only then can other guests leave.

Under no circumstances should cameras be taken to formal royal occasions.

Diplomatic functions

Diplomatic functions will often be attended by guests of several different nationalities. If you are not sure of the particular rules of etiquette observed by other nationalities, check with the embassy that has invited you or with the protocol department of any other relevant embassy. Many diplomatic functions are very formal and will require men to wear black or white tie (or uniform, national or clerical dress). If the invitation specifies informal wear, this should not be interpreted literally: it actually means that men should wear lounge suits. (See **Correct Clothes** in the Basic Rules section.)

FUNERALS AND MEMORIALS

Losing a loved one is a most painful and distressing experience, and the fact that we no longer have a ritual period of mourning may make it even more difficult for the bereaved to come to terms with their altered lives. Arranging a funeral can make this period still more difficult to bear or it may alleviate some of the anguish. If a death was predictable, some of the arrangements may have been made in advance – this is not morbid, but practical.

Registering deaths

Sometimes a doctor is present when a person dies, for example if he or she is in hospital, otherwise a doctor should be contacted immediately. If the person carries a donor card, a hospital should also be informed as quickly as possible.

The doctor will supply a death certificate unless for any reason the death is reported to the coroner for a post mortem or an inquest; the coroner would then give his authority for the certificate. Within two weeks of the death (eight days in Scotland) this certificate should be taken to the register office to register the death. This should be done by the next of kin, if possible, because the register office will need to know many details about the deceased, such as his or her full name (including a married woman's maiden name), address, occupation and details about his or her family.

It is also a good idea to contact the bank of the deceased and to inform any credit card companies for which he or she holds cards. Get in touch with his or her solicitor and find out if there is a will.

Making a will

A will need not be a long and complicated document, but it is a great help to the family of the bereaved. The estate of someone who dies without leaving a will is divided according to the intestacy laws. These laws aim to distribute an estate according to the deceased's presumed wish that he or she would want the property to benefit their closest relatives. These laws, however, were written many years ago and society has changed considerably, for instance more people now own their own homes, and there is more divorce, remarriage and cohabitation. In consequence, these laws formulated in a past social context when applied in today's may seem arbitrary and clumsy. So the best thing to do is to avoid this situation by making a will.

Solicitors can advise you how to make a will, and can draw one up for you. Many people first make a will when they get married or when they have children, and they may change their will periodically during their lives.

The truly thoughtful give some idea in their will of what sort of funeral arrangements they would like, and they may leave money specifically to cover for these arrangements. If you would like your will to include rather eccentric instructions for your burial, take the precaution of checking how much it will all cost and how easily it can be arranged. The next of kin are actually not legally bound to obey these burial instructions.

Letting people know

People close to the deceased who will be distressed to hear of his or her death, should be informed as quickly as possible and preferably in person. If this is not possible you should try to make sure that someone is close by to comfort them and check that they are all right when you ring or write with the news. If you yourself are too moved by the death to deal with other people, find someone else to let friends and relations know.

SPECIAL OCCASIONS

If you tell someone about a death, be prepared for any sort of reaction. Some people are very emotional and restless, others may be utterly silent and apparently unmoved – we all have different ways of dealing with our grief. Ask the person whether he or she would like to be left alone or would like you to stay. If you stay, you may not need to talk – just being there may be a comfort to someone in the shock of grief.

When you hear of someone's death, don't be shy about getting in touch with his or her grieving next of kin. People are so unsure of how to deal with other people's pain that the bereaved are often left alone and they feel even more isolated. Get in touch or go and see him or her, see whether there is anything you can do to help. Be sensitive to the needs of the bereaved: if you feel that you are intruding, eclipse yourself. Often it is best just to be there with him or her, not talking or doing very much, simply listening when he or she wants to speak.

Death announcements may be put in national or local newspapers, although this is not necessary. If you would like to put an announcement in a paper, check with the paper of your choice for the usual layout of the announcements. You may simply wish to announce the death or you may choose to mention the time and the place of the funeral, cremation or memorial service. Many people prefer mourners to give donations to charity than to send flowers to the funeral; this can be made clear in the announcement. Similarly, if the bereaved family feel they cannot cope with letters of condolence they may choose to put 'no letters' at the end of the announcement.

Letters of condolence
Letters of condolence are difficult to write but they can be a great comfort. They should be written as soon as possible, but they may well continue to give comfort many weeks or even months after the death. Try to write as naturally as possible, preferably

including an anecdote which illustrates the fond memories you have of the deceased.

Offer your support to the bereaved in your letter, and let him or her know that you don't expect a reply. If he or she is numbed and disorientated by grief it may be a relief not to be faced with having to write scores of letters. On the other hand, it won't stop the bereaved from writing back if he or she is lonely and longing for things to fill the time.

If you receive letters of condolence you should reply to every one and thank the people who sent them. If you feel you can't deal with this task, try to find someone else to do it for you, or have some cards typed or printed with a message of thanks.

Funeral directors

Funeral directors can be found by looking in the local yellow pages. They should be contacted as soon as possible, but they will not be able to take the body from you or the hospital until you have a death certificate.

Don't worry if you feel inefficient or confused in your dealings with the funeral directors; they are used to working for the bereaved and they may take many anxieties off your shoulders. Undertakers can take care of every aspect of the burial including contacting solicitors, printing service sheets, arranging for announcements to appear in newspapers, booking the church and dealing with the digging of a grave. They will also ask you where you would like the body to be kept before the funeral or cremation. Some families like the body to stay at home; others prefer it to be kept on the undertaker's premises; it is more common for the body to be kept in a chapel of rest, where it can be visited.

The main anxiety many families have with respect to funeral directors is that of expense. It is up to you how much you spend on the arrangements, unless of course provision has been made for them in the will. A lavish funeral with an expensive coffin and a long cortege of hired cars does not show any more affection for the deceased than a more discreet ceremony. Many of the expenses of a funeral are actually avoidable; for example it is not in fact a legal requirement to have a religious ceremony at all – the deceased can simply be buried in accordance with local authority regulations. The coffin need not even be carried by hired bearers if there are enough strong men among the mourners who are prepared to show this final respect to the deceased, or a purpose-made trolley may be available.

Funeral arrangements

It is not necessary, and there is usually not time, to send invitations to a funeral. Some families prefer funerals to be very small and intimate, others may let friends know when the funeral will be or they may include details of the service in a newspaper announcement.

The arrangements for getting the coffin and the chief mourners to the church should be made with the funeral directors. The funeral should be held in the deceased's local parish church or a church which he or she attended regularly. The order of service should be discussed with the incumbent vicar; if you would like a different vicar to take the service or to contribute to it, you should discuss this idea diplomatically with the incumbent vicar.

On the day of the funeral the undertakers arrange for the coffin to be delivered to the church. If the coffin has been kept at home, the officiating vicar may be invited to say a few prayers before it leaves the house. Close family and friends form the cortege of cars immediately behind the hearse on the way to the church. Black, chauffeur-driven cars may be hired, but many families prefer to use their own cars.

Funeral services are usually fairly short, and most of the service is held inside the church. The coffin is laid on a stand at the front of the church and the front pews are reserved for the immediate family. A close relation should always escort the chief mourner throughout the proceedings to support and comfort him or her; for example a widow might be accompanied by her brother or her eldest son.

After the church service the coffin is taken to the graveside for the brief ceremony of interment. This is often attended only by close family, although sometimes the entire congregation gathers around the grave. Following the interment those who have attended the funeral should go to the chief mourner to offer their sympathy. For cremations, the coffin is taken from the church to the crematorium where a brief committal service is held (it may be possible to have a committal service at the door of the church, but check first).

A member of the family or an employee of the funeral director should collect the cards on the bouquets by the graveside for the chief mourner, who may draw comfort from them and may wish to write and thank for them.

Attending funerals

Although people no longer wear only black at funerals, it is a sign of respect to wear sober colours with only discreet jewellery. Some men wear a black tie or a black armband, and women may like to wear a hat, possibly with a veil. If you are likely to be tearful during the service, a veil can make it difficult to deal with your tears discreetly.

Some families discourage the sending of flowers or ask people to make a donation to charity instead; if this is the case you should respect their wishes. If not, flowers are usually sent either to the relevant undertaker or to the house of the next of kin on the morning of the funeral, or you may wish to take flowers with you to place by the grave. You should put a small card with the flowers with a personal note from yourself to the deceased. Only flowers given by the immediate family are put on the coffin.

Cremations

Some people are squeamish about the idea of cremation, so it is worth remembering that you must not cremate a body if the deceased did not stipulate cremation in his or her will; on the other hand you are under no legal obligation to cremate the body if he or she did. In order to have a body cremated you will need two doctor's certificates (or a coroner's certificate if the death was referred to the coroner) as well as a signed certificate from the medical representative at the crematorium and a signed application form from the next of kin.

Crematoria are usually small, and cremations are traditionally attended only by immediate family and very close friends. Most crematoria are non-denominational – although many can recommend a Church of England vicar to take the service. The family may invite a clergyman of their choice to officiate, or a cremation need not involve a religious ceremony at all.

The ashes may be buried at the crematorium, in which case a small space has to be bought; they may be interred in a graveyard – perhaps in the grave of a close relation or even a family grave; they may be scattered; or they may be kept in an urn.

Those who attend cremations should be quiet even before and after the ceremony: there may be another cremation taking place immediately before or after the one you are attending and it would be very distressing for the mourners to hear people chatting outside the little chapel. As with funerals, people tend to wear dark clothes at cremations and many women choose to wear hats. Flowers are not usually brought to cremations unless the casket is to be buried at the crematorium. Small bouquets from the immediate family are usually laid on the coffin.

Memorial services

A memorial service may be called a service of remembrance or, in the Roman Catholic faith, a Requiem Mass. Such services are usually held a few days or weeks after the funeral or cremation and they are generally held as a celebration of the life and achievements of a person of some import – although, not necessarily on an international scale.

If you arrange to have a newspaper announcement just after a death you may mention in the announcement that a memorial service will be held, giving the time, date and place. You may like to invite people individually either by telephoning, writing or even sending printed invitations.

Memorial services are usually held in the local church of the deceased or a church that he or she attended regularly. The family should discuss the order of the service and the choice of music, hymns, prayers and readings with the vicar; they may choose to have service sheets printed. If they would like to invite another vicar to participate in or take the service they should make sure that this is acceptable to the incumbent vicar.

If you are invited to – or choose to – attend a memorial service, you should be smartly and soberly dressed, but not gloomily so; memorial services are often uplifting occasions, intended as celebrations.

Refreshments

After a funeral, cremation or memorial service the chief mourner or a close friend may invite other mourners for some form of refreshment. Many people travel considerable distances to pay their last respects; they may welcome the opportunity to relax before their return journey, and to spend some time with the other mourners.

It is up to the family to choose whether they arrange a formal meal for a set number of people in a restaurant, or whether they casually invite anyone and everyone attending the service to join them for a drink. The atmosphere at such occasions depends to some extent on the setting and the mood of the chief mourner, but – although it would be disrespectful to be riotous – it need not be cheerless.

FUNERALS AND MEMORIALS CHECKLIST

Important dos and don'ts

✓ **DO make a will and keep it up-to-date**
✓ **DO contact close friends and relatives**
✓ **DO offer support or condolences to the bereaved**
✗ **DON'T expect replies or acknowledgements from the bereaved**
✗ **DON'T send flowers if asked not to**
✗ **DON'T worry about funeral arrangements – let funeral directors take care of the details**

HOUSE GUESTS

Having people to stay can be great fun and it is a good way to get to know your friends better, but you should plan carefully before inviting house guests. There is a Spanish proverb which runs something along the lines of, 'after three days fish and visitors stink'; it is worth bearing in mind that – however fond you are of someone – having them in your own home 24 hours a day can be quite taxing.

The invitation

Inviting house guests need not be a formal business, it may be easiest to invite them over the telephone so that you can discuss all the details. Make it clear when you would like them to arrive and when you expect them to leave. If they are travelling by public transport this should be easy because you can suggest to meet them off a particular train or bus.

When you invite people to stay give them a clear idea of what you have planned for their stay, so that they will know what to bring with them. Let them know if they should bring smart clothes for a dance or dinner party, and/or if they will need outdoor clothes. You may want them to bring tennis rackets or swimming things or just a good book if you are planning a relaxing time.

If you know the guests well it may be easy just to laze around while they are staying, but if you are inviting people you don't know well it is best to have something planned: a drinks party, a trip to a local historic building, a game of tennis – the choice is yours. On the other hand, don't overwhelm your guests with a hectic schedule of activities; respect the fact that they have routines of their own and that they may want to relax.

Accepting an invitation

If you accept an invitation to go and stay with someone but are not sure whether the invitation includes your children, or you would like to take your pet, always check with your hosts first. Try to word the question so that they feel they can say no to you, rather than forcing them by saying 'you don't mind if I bring the cat, do you?' (See also **Children** and **Pets** in the Basic Rules section.)

When you accept the invitation make sure you know when you are expected to arrive and to leave, and get some idea of what you are likely to be doing during your stay, so that you know what to pack. When you reply you should also let your hosts know if you have any special dietary requirement.

Preparing a room

The bedroom your guests are going to use should always be prepared in time for their arrival. The room should be warm but well aired; the bed should be made (with spare blankets available in case they are needed); towels and drinking water should be provided; and cupboard space with hangers made available. Many hosts also like to put flowers in the room, and to provide biscuits, magazines and even a radio. If the room or just the cupboard space is used by a member of the family, try to make sure that everything he or she might need from the room is taken out before the guests arrive so that they are not disturbed during their stay.

If you invite an unmarried couple that you don't know very well you may not be sure how to deal with their sleeping arrangements. Some hosts may prefer to put such guests in separate bedrooms. Others take the plunge and put them in the same room – although it would be advisable to give them twin beds not a double bed. The best solution is for the hosts to check with the girl whether she would like to be put in the same room as her boyfriend. However, it is your house, and if you don't approve of unmarried couples sleeping together they must appreciate your wishes.

The arrival

It is important not to arrive early if you have been invited to stay with friends; they may have quite a lot of preparations to do, and may not appreciate you turning up while the house is still in pandemonium. You should, however, make an effort to arrive on time, especially if you have been asked to arrive in time for a meal.

You may like to bring a gift for your hosts with you. If you know them well you will know what they would most appreciate, whether it be a bottle of whisky or a houseplant. If you don't know your hosts well, you may prefer to get to know them during your stay and send them an appropriate present afterwards as a token of thanks. In any event, there is nothing to say that you have to arrive bearing a gift.

As soon as guests arrive they should be shown to their rooms and shown where the bathroom is, so that they can drop off their bags and freshen up. This is especially true if they have had a long journey. If there is only one bathroom, this is a good time for hosts to let their guests know at what times the bathroom is likely to be free. It might be a good idea to let them know where the iron and ironing board are too. Guests should be left alone to unpack their bags and settle in, and they should be told how soon they are expected back downstairs – allow them time to settle in, but don't leave them stranded.

SPECIAL OCCASIONS

Looking after guests

Hosts should try to provide their guests with everything they are likely to need, and should allow for them to stick to some extent to their own daily routines. This is especially true if the guest is elderly or accompanied by young children. If guests offer to help, hosts should try to find something that they can do rather than abandoning them while they – the hosts – toil in the kitchen.

If you have exuberant children or pets, try to keep them under control so that they don't disturb or upset your guests. If your guests bring children or pets make sure that they have everything they need. If they bring a baby, it is best to ask the mother in advance what she will need, and offer her the use of the washing machine while she is staying.

Have plenty of things planned for your guests but give them time to relax; the more flexible you are the more enjoyable their stay is likely to be. Let them know if you like to have certain meals at particular times or if you tend to go to bed especially early or late. Don't feel that every meal has to be a great feast; for example, casual breakfasts can be one of the great pleasures of a house party. Just let everyone know at what sort of time they should emerge for breakfast, and provide enough food (whether it is just toast and marmalade or a full English breakfast) for everyone to help themselves.

Earning your keep

House guests should always bear in mind that their hosts go to considerable trouble to put them up. Guests can reciprocate for this effort by observing a few simple rules.

Guests should always respect the host's house, belongings and routine: they should not raid the fridge, lie full length on the only sofa or keep their hosts up all night if they are quite obviously exhausted. Good guests will try to avoid sitting in someone's favourite chair, or using the bathroom at someone's usual time. They should also respect the host's morals: if you have not been put in the same bedroom as your boyfriend or girlfriend, you should not slip along the corridor during the night.

When you stay in someone else's house, you should always make your bed in the morning, keep your room tidy and be scrupulous in cleaning the bathroom after use. You should also offer to help, for example, with the cooking; part of the fun of a house party is joining in with its administration. If, on the other hand, your hosts would rather do all the work themselves, make sure you have a good book to read so that they don't feel you are getting bored while you wait.

Contribute to everyone's enjoyment by wholeheartedly joining in any activities that may have been organized for you. If you can, and without forcing the issue, make financial contributions, for example, paying for a meal out or a sporting activity. If your hosts insist on paying don't argue with them as this would appear ungrateful. When you are offered things, try to give yes or no answers: if something has been offered you can only assume that your hosts are prepared to give it to you so don't feel you are being a burden to them. Don't say 'I don't mind' or 'only if you're making one anyway'; these sort of noncommittal answers can be very frustrating for a host who would genuinely like to please you.

If you take children or pets with you, try to keep them under control at all times and make sure that you take everything they need with you. Try not to ask for things while you are staying with friends unless there is something you really need. Certainly don't use the telephone without asking, and always offer to pay if you have to make any calls.

SPECIAL OCCASIONS

Leaving and thanking

On the last morning of your stay, take the bed linen off and fold it neatly with the towels you have used. Always try to leave at the time you and your hosts agreed when they first invited you: having people to stay is quite an effort and, however much your hosts appear to be relishing your stay, they will be grateful to you for leaving at the agreed time, especially if they have to go to work the following day.

It goes without saying that, as you leave, you should thank your hosts for having you to stay. Very soon afterwards you should also write to thank them; a telephone call would not be adequate. You may like to send them flowers or a small gift as a token of thanks. If you took photographs during your stay, you might even order a second set of prints and send one set to your hosts.

HOUSE GUESTS – CHECKLIST

Important dos and don'ts

✓ **DO make it clear how long you are inviting someone**
✓ **DO say what activities, if any, there will be**
✓ **DO be a helpful and enthusiastic guest**
✓ **DO write and thank your hosts**
✗ **DON'T bring children and pets without asking first**
✗ **DON'T be too self-effacing, but don't treat the place like home**
✗ **DON'T overstay your welcome**

INTERVIEW TECHNIQUE

A job interview can be a daunting experience with a great deal at stake for the interviewee. Unfortunately, nerves are almost inevitable and they do not act in favour of the interviewee. But if he or she is well prepared the interview should go more smoothly and nerves may not be so much of a problem. It is always best to find out as much as possible about the company you are being interviewed by and about the job for which you are applying. This will help you understand the questions asked and should arm you with some intelligent questions to ask in turn. Interview etiquette revolves around honesty, a show of confidence and common courtesy.

What to wear

The type of job you are applying for will obviously have considerable bearing on what you choose to wear. You should think about whether your interview is going to be held in an executive's office or on the factory floor. Most interviews take place in an office and in these circumstances the interviewee should be smartly dressed; men should wear suits or at least a jacket and tie, and women should choose comparably smart clothes – a suit or dress.

However smart your clothes are you should not let them smother your character. Men can hint at their more eccentric or imaginative streak by their choice of tie, by having a brightly coloured handkerchief in their top pocket, or simply by the colour of their socks. Women can achieve the same effect with accessories and jewellery, although ornate or very showy jewellery can be off-putting. While women should not deliberately choose dowdy clothes for interviews, they should avoid wearing overtly sexy clothes.

In short, interview clothes should say something about yourself while helping you to exude an air of confidence and professionalism. The most important thing about interview clothes is that they should be comfortable. If you buy an outfit especially for an interview, make sure you wear it in first so that it is comfortable and feels familiar.

Arriving for interviews

You should always leave time to arrive punctually at interviews, but do not arrive early. If you have time to spare, spend it collecting your thoughts before presenting yourself for the interview. If you present yourself too early you will appear a little desperate and insecure, and you will give yourself time to get nervous while you sit and wait. While you are waiting to go into your interview take a few deep breaths to calm yourself and think over the questions you would like to ask your interviewer.

When your interviewer arrives or when you are shown into his or her office, smile and make eye contact. If he or she offers a hand to shake, take it firmly but don't wag it briskly. Make sure you get the interviewer's name, and use it at intervals during the interview. If you are offered a cup of tea or coffee, don't resort to saying, 'I don't mind' or 'only if you're having one'; although accommodating, these are indecisive replies that will not impress a prospective employer. Whether or not your interviewer is drinking anything, it is a good idea to accept the offer of a drink; this is an indication that you feel comfortable, and having the drink may help you to relax.

Talking shop

The main object of an interview is for the prospective employer to let you know about the job in question and to size you up. If the interviewer talks at length, concentrate on what he or she is saying: everything the interviewer tells you about the job should help you to plead your own case as a prospective employee. If you concentrate, you won't be caught out if he or she suddenly says 'do you agree?'.

If you disagree with something the interviewer has said, say so (always remember that he or she may have deliberately said something contentious to see whether you had the nerve to stick to your opinion). Be yourself and be honest about yourself; if you have to lie or change yourself to get a job, you are unlikely to be successful or happy in it. Give honest answers to questions even if you think you are not saying what the interviewer wants to hear; it is better to say 'this may not be what you want to hear, but . . .' than to lie.

When the interviewer asks you a difficult question, don't be afraid to take your time in answering. You may even give them a wry smile or admit 'that's a difficult one', but don't let yourself be rushed into answering straight away.

Never forget that you are sizing the company up just as much as they are sizing you up. You should always have questions ready to ask them. A lack of interest and curiosity in the company and the job would not be a good sign. But you should not ask questions about working hours and time off; that would indicate a negative attitude to the work.

Leaving an interview

At the end of the interview the interviewer will usually thank you for coming, and will say that the company will be getting in touch to let you know whether or not you have the job. This is your cue to leave, and you should not linger on after it. As you get to your feet, you should thank the interviewer for agreeing to see you and make a final remark about how much you would enjoy being a part of the company.

Try to put your hand forward to shake hands before the interviewer does; this is a positive, assertive gesture. As you leave the room, don't just walk out and close the door behind you, but turn round and offer them one last smile before you leave.

INTERVIEW ETIQUETTE – CHECKLIST

Important dos and don'ts

✓ **DO be smartly but soberly dressed, don't overdress**
✓ **DO arrive on time, but try not to be too early**
✓ **DO smile and make eye contact with the interviewer**
✓ **DO think of your own questions to ask**
X **DON'T panic, try to control your nerves and relax**
X **DON'T say the first thing that comes into your head**
X **DON'T slouch or mumble when you speak**

PARTIES AND ENTERTAINING

There are many different ways of entertaining guests less formally than at a dinner party. You may choose to give a drinks party, a buffet lunch or a dancing party. These occasions will require considerable forward planning, particularly if you are expecting a large number of guests. For some of the key rules about entertaining, see Dinner Parties in this section.

Planning larger parties

Whatever sort of party you decide to organize, you will need to begin planning some time in advance. Invitations should go out about three weeks in advance for drinks parties and buffet parties, and about a month in advance for dancing parties.

When you draw up your guest list, bear in mind that usually only about 70% of people asked are free to come to parties (slightly fewer in summer when people are away on holiday, or at Christmas when there are many parties). This means that you can invite over the odds on numbers in order to ensure that the party feels full. If there are not enough people for the amount of space available the party may fall a little flat.

If you are asking large numbers of people, you need not worry so much about who you invite with whom; if you have two friends who are bound to disagree, they will be perfectly able to avoid each other. Similarly, it does not matter if there are a few more men than women or vice versa.

Drinks parties

Evening or pre-lunch drinks parties are a good way of introducing your friends to each other, and of extending an invitation to new friends and casual acquaintances. Most drinks parties last a couple of hours; if you want people to leave at a particular time – in order to go on to give some of the guests a meal, for example – you should make this clear on the invitation. Daytime parties can be from 12 noon until 2pm and evening parties from 6.30 till 8.30. You may of course want the people to stay on longer, in which case you need only state a starting time on your invitation.

Make sure that you have enough drink and nearly twice as many glasses as there are guests; when people move around they tend to put glasses down and then pick up a new one. It is best not to use your best glasses when entertaining larger numbers of people, and if you don't have enough glasses of your own many wine merchants will loan out glasses – often free of charge – if you buy your drink from them.

What drink you choose to give your guests is entirely up to you. The more people you have invited, the more simple the choice should be. You might want to offer just red or white wine, or one cocktail that you have made up in large quantities in advance. You should always offer soft drinks as an alternative. When guests are arriving, it is easiest to have trays of drinks already poured to offer them; and as the party progresses you (or your helpers, if you have any) can circulate with bottles or jugs to top up glasses.

People should always be offered something to eat with a drink. It is up to you and your culinary skills whether you give them just crisps and nuts or elaborate canapés. If you are expecting people to leave and go on to eat later, the food need not be particularly substantial. Food can either be handed round or left in strategic places around the room.

Buffet parties

Buffet parties are a practical way of feeding a large number of people in an informal atmosphere. They can be held at lunch time, in which case guests should be invited for 12.30 or 1.00 pm, or in the evening, in which case the invitation should be for 7.30 or 8.00 pm.

Make sure that you have enough room to feed all of the people that you have invited, and that at least some of them can sit. Check also that you have enough cutlery, crockery and serving dishes for the occasion. It is unwise to use the best dinner service for a buffet party; you may even want to use paper plates and plastic cutlery.

Prepare the room or rooms in advance so that there are a number of chairs and little tables scattered around for people to use. This is particularly important if you have invited children, who will not be used to balancing plates of food, or elderly guests, who may not want to remain standing for too long.

The buffet table should, as far as possible, be laid in advance so that you are free to welcome your guests, give them a drink and introduce them to each other. If it is in the same room that guests first come into you may want to cover it with a large cloth until it is time to eat – usually about 45 minutes after the first guests arrived. Lay the table with plates at one end, food in the middle and cutlery at the far end so that guests move one way along the table. The food should be laid out so that guests arrive at the main dish or dishes first, then side dishes (such as salad or vegetables), then extras (such as garlic bread), sauces and condiments.

The choice of food depends to some extent on how many of your guests are going to be able to sit down. It is impossible to stand and cut food up with a knife and fork so, if not everyone is to be seated, the food should be easy to eat with a fork or even with just fingers. Hot dishes with rice and pasta can be eaten with a fork and cold quiches can be cut up in advance into individual portions. Most buffet parties consist of only a main course or a main course followed by dessert or cheese.

SPECIAL OCCASIONS

Drinks should probably be served in the same way as for drinks parties above, or you may choose to have a separate table as a bar so that guests can help themselves. It is easiest to offer a simple choice of drinks, such as red or white wine, and soft drinks.

Dancing parties

If you invite people for an evening of dancing the invitation should be for 9.00 pm onwards (some dances and balls begin at 10.00 pm) unless you are also providing a meal in which case you may want to ask people for 8.00 pm. If you are providing food, it is best to serve a buffet supper in a separate room or area, away from the dance floor. Even if food is not provided it is sometimes a good idea to have a separate room where people can relax and chat in relative quiet.

At dancing parties it is particularly important to make sure that you have invited enough guests to fill the space; if there are too few guests, they may feel shy and it may be difficult to start people dancing. If you hire a space, such as a hall, you may be able to make a more intimate atmosphere by dimming the lighting and adding a false ceiling so that the room does not feel so large.

It is usual to offer guests a choice of wine or beer, and of course soft drinks. If you would like people to bring a bottle with them, say so on the invitation, otherwise you can't rely on them to do so. Do make sure that you have more than enough for your guests to drink; few things kill a party more quickly than a dry bar. Many wine merchants will let you buy drink on a sale or return basis and they may even throw in the hire of glasses free of charge.

The best way to serve the drink is to have a large table as a bar. As each guest arrives take him or her to the 'bar' and pour them their first drink and let them know that they can help themselves from then on, unless of course you have hired bar staff. Even if you are not serving a meal, you may like to lay on a small amount of food: just crisps and nuts, or a late-night barbecue, or – if the party is intended to go on very late – an early morning breakfast.

PARTIES & ENTERTAINING – CHECKLIST

Important dos and don'ts

✓ **DO plan well in advance**
✓ **DO specify times and whether food will be provided**
✓ **DO make sure that you have enough drink, and always have soft drinks available**
✓ **DO make sure you invite enough people; too many is better than too few**
X **DON'T cram your guests into one room, make sure they can move about easily**
X **DON'T use your best crockery and glasses**

RESTAURANT MEALS

Eating out in restaurants is a very pleasant way of entertaining whether socially or professionally. It is of course more expensive than entertaining at home, but it involves none of the hard work. If you are organizing a restaurant meal you should always book the table in advance and, if you are inviting a large party, arrange your seating plan beforehand.

Inviting and paying

It should be clear at the time of the invitation who will be paying for a restaurant meal. If you agree to go out for a meal with friends you should share the bill. The cost should simply be divided by the number of people eating rather than each person working out how much their meal was worth. However, if one person ate fewer courses or drank no alcohol, the other members of the party should offer for them to pay less.

If you invite someone out for a meal, you should pay for it. Conversely, if you are invited out for a meal there should not be any need for you to offer to pay. Some girls like to split the cost of a meal if they are invited out by a man they do not know very well because they do not like to feel indebted to him. In any event you should never argue about paying the bill when it arrives, and a girl should never feel she owes anything to a man just because he has insisted on paying for her meal.

What to wear

What you wear to a restaurant depends only to a small extent on the establishment itself: some very smart restaurants or the dining rooms of certain clubs and hotels may stipulate that men wear a tie or they may even require evening dress after 6 pm. In most cases, the choice is yours, and you should agree what to wear with the person or people you have invited for the meal so that no-one feels under- or overdressed. Choose your restaurant carefully if your party is, for example, casually dressed because you are going on to an outdoor pop concert or, alternatively, fantastically elegant in preparation for a formal ball.

When to arrive

A lunch time meal will usually be booked for between 12.30 and 1.00 pm, and an evening meal any time between 7.30 and 9.00 pm. If you are eating after attending some event or are going on to do something else, you should check how early or how late the restaurant takes bookings, and ensure that they have noted your booking time.

If you have invited a friend or friends to a restaurant, you should always arrive a little early so that they do not have to wait for you. Make a particular point of arriving early if your guest is a woman; it can be awkward and embarrassing for a woman to wait alone in a restaurant.

Those invited to eat out should arrive promptly so that their host is not kept waiting and does not, therefore, run the risk of losing his or her reservation or annoying the staff by altering it. If the party of diners arrive together the host or party leader should enter the restaurant first and ask for his or her table.

Ordering your meal

Most menus offer a choice of dishes, this is known as an à la carte menu; others may offer a set menu or table d'hôte at a fixed price, this is a set meal which may give you one or two choices. Before ordering your meal you should establish how many courses the other members of the party are intending to have. If there is anything on the menu that you don't understand or would like to

SPECIAL OCCASIONS

know more about, ask your waiter. If you are a guest, you should ask your host to ask the waiter. Very large parties may agree on a choice of menu and order it in advance.

The waiter will initially take orders for the first course and main course. When the main course has been cleared he will return to take orders for dessert and/or cheese, and coffee. Traditionally, the party leader orders the meal, having asked each of the guests what he or she would like to eat. It is more common, however, for the waiter to ask each diner in turn for his or her order. Even so, it is considered polite for guests to let their host know what they would like to eat before ordering it.

When someone asks you out for a meal, some people would say that it is rude to choose either the cheapest or the most expensive dish on the menu. It is of course unfair to select something very expensive if everyone else is having more modest dishes, but if you are invited to choose whatever you would like it is most polite to do just that. In some restaurants ladies may be given menus without prices; if this happens to you and you are afraid of ordering a terribly expensive dish, bear in mind that sirloin steak, shellfish and certain fish (such as salmon and monkfish) are likely to be highly priced.

If you would like something that is not on the menu you should ask your waiter very politely, but not make a scene if he is unable to help you. In general, cheaper restaurants and franchise restaurants will not be able to provide things that are not on the menu. More expensive establishments that make everything from fresh ingredients may find it easier to oblige.

Wine and drinks

In many restaurants diners are asked if they would like an aperitif before their meal. If you have been invited by someone else, check whether he or she will be having an aperitif before asking for one, because this may add considerably to the final bill.

The wine and drinks list may be separate to the menu and it may be presented to the host alone. The host should choose a wine and let his or her guest or guests know of this choice before ordering it. If you have been asked out for a meal don't be afraid to say if you would prefer not to drink wine.

The wine should be brought to the table in its unopened bottle unless you order a carafe. The waiter will show you the label before opening the bottle and will then pour a small amount into the host's glass. Tasting the wine should be done quickly and without fuss; this is not an opportunity for you to decide you don't like the wine you have chosen, but to see whether or not the wine is corked. There may be tiny pieces of cork floating in the wine – this is quite common and does the wine no harm at all. Corked wine, on the other hand, is rare; it smells and tastes very sour and should be rejected. Once the person tasting the wine has approved it, he or she should ask the waiter to pour the wine.

During the meal

When eating in a restaurant diners should observe the same courtesies as when invited to eat at someone else's house (see **Dinner Parties** in this section and **Table Manners** in Basic Rules). They should also remember that they are not the only clients in the restaurant. However much you are enjoying a meal with a group of friends you should not become rowdy at the expense of other clients.

You should also be especially attentive to the fact that other people may not like you to smoke while they are eating; some restaurants have no-smoking areas, others forbid smoking altogether. If you are sitting very close to the next table and would like to smoke, you should ask the people at the next table if they would mind.

Although people do not usually leave the table during a dinner party, it is generally considered acceptable to go to the toilet during a restaurant meal. If you want to go to the toilet, wait for the end of a course, excuse yourself quietly and return as quickly as possible.

Waiters and waitresses

Waiting staff should always be treated courteously; they are professionals, not servants and their service will be better if you treat them as such. Never whistle, call or snap your fingers at waiters or waitresses across the room – however diligently they are ignoring you! You should attract their attention by catching their eye, raising your hand or saying 'excuse me' as they pass near you. If he or she still fails to come over to your table, or if there is anything else about the service that displeases you, go over and tell the person discreetly and emphatically what the problem is rather than making a scene in front of your guest or guests.

Some waiting staff can be intimidating, especially to those who are not accustomed to eating in restaurants. However unsure you feel, always remember that you are the customer and therefore have the upper hand: you are not obliged to pay for service if you feel that it has been unsatisfactory.

Complaining

Some people complain all too readily in restaurants others are so afraid to do so that even vegetarians would chomp through a steak tartare served in error! You should not be embarrassed about complaining if you have a genuine reason to do so, on the other hand few problems that arise during the course of a restaurant meal warrant a real scene. If you would like to complain about something it is best to leave your table – therefore avoiding embarrassing your guest or guests – and talk to the waiting staff or the manager.

Only in really extreme circumstances should you refuse to pay for your meal; and you should never refuse to pay for a meal after completing it. If something about the meal, the restaurant or the staff makes you feel unwilling to pay for your meal, you should stop eating immediately and make your feelings known. Most establishments will try to mollify you by offering you part of the meal or perhaps the drink on the house; if at all possible you should accept this graciously and continue with the meal.

The bill

When the bill is brought to the table the person who is to pay for it – or who has decided to do the mathematics for a party of diners – should signal to the waiter and take the bill from him. He or she should check it over briefly but not pick through it in fine detail unless the total is very wide of the anticipated mark.

If it is not clear whether service has been included in the total, the host should ask the waiting staff. Unless you were particularly displeased with the service you should add a tip of 10 or

---

RESTAURANT MEALS – CHECKLIST

Important dos and don'ts

✓ **DO make sure that it is understood who is paying**
✓ **DO be at the restaurant before your guests**
✓ **DO complain if you are unhappy, but be discreet and polite**
✗ **DON'T treat the staff as servants, but equally don't be intimidated**
✗ **DON'T become too noisy or rowdy**

SPECIAL OCCASIONS

15% when a service charge has not been included. If you are paying by credit card the waiting staff may leave the total column open in the hope that you will add a tip to the subtotal. You may choose to tip them in this way, but most waiters and waitresses prefer cash tips.

THEATRE TRIPS AND OTHER OUTINGS

Trips to the theatre, opera, ballet, concerts and cinema are a very agreeable way of spending an evening and of entertaining friends. One golden rule to remember when attending any public performance, is that each member of the audience should make every effort not to inconvenience those around him or her, nor to distract the performers.

Planning the evening

Most evening performances begin between 7.00 and 8.00 pm, which may give people little time to change after work. It is, therefore, best to arrange to meet up only shortly before the performance is due to begin. At the weekend you may decide to make more of a party of it, and arrange to have drinks or an early meal somewhere before hand.

Some theatres provide snacks during the interval, and you and the other member or members of the party should decide whether you would like to eat before, during or after the performance. There are usually a number of restaurants near theatres and opera houses that are used to taking late-night bookings; some even offer a special after-show menu.

Who pays for the tickets?

When two or more friends agree to go to a show it is usually easiest if one person pays for the tickets and is then paid back by the others. Most theatres accept credit card bookings, which means that the party organizer need not be out of pocket until he or she is paid back.

SPECIAL OCCASIONS

If you are invited to a performance, this usually means that the person inviting you intends to pay for your ticket. In order to be sure, you might want to ask him or her 'would you like me to pay for my ticket'. If your host refuses you should thank him or her warmly both at the time of asking and on the evening itself. If you feel you would like to reciprocate, you could either invite your host out for a meal afterwards or to another show at a later date. If this is not within your means you should make a point of buying a programme for the show and of offering your host a drink during the interval.

What to wear

It is no longer a requirement of theatres that the audience wear evening dress, so what you wear depends on who you go with and, perhaps, how much you paid for your tickets. At the Royal Opera House in Covent Garden, for example, spectators in the stalls, the circle and the boxes are usually dressed formally, whilst those peering down from the amphitheatre may well be in jeans. Audiences do, however, tend to dress more formally for ballet and opera than for the theatre and concerts. At Glyndeborne it is customary to wear evening dress.

If you want to make an outing of a trip to the cinema, there is nothing to stop you dressing up for it; on the other hand, if you regularly attend the ballet you may not feel the need to dress up for a full, classical ballet. When you organize an outing to a show with a friend or friends make sure that you let them know what you will be wearing so that they can dress accordingly.

Arriving

Unless you are held up by unforeseen circumstances don't arrive at the theatre at the very last minute and hope that you will meet up easily with the rest of your party. Theatre foyers are crowded, noisy places. It is better to arrange to meet up for a quick drink near to the theatre, especially if you are one of a large party.

When you take your seat in the auditorium you should thank those who have to move or stand to let you pass; make sure that you have everything you need – such as programmes or ice creams – so that you do not have to disturb them again until the interval. If someone needs to squeeze past you to get to his or her seat, stand up and move any bags or belongings out of the narrow gangway.

If someone else appears to be in your seat, ask politely if you can see his or her ticket. Similarly, if someone thinks that the seat you are sitting in is his or hers, check your ticket. If the other person refuses to move or if you need any further help, refer the problem to an usher or usherette rather than causing a scene. It goes without saying that if you were in the wrong you should apologize to the other person.

The rules governing late arrivals vary with each production. If you arrive after the curtain has gone up you may have to wait for a suitable pause in the action, such as the end of a scene; but you may not be allowed into the auditorium until the interval. The only way to avoid this disappointment is to make sure that you arrive on time. If you do arrive late and are forbidden access to the auditorium until a given point in the performance, don't argue with ushers. When you are allowed to go to your seat, do so as quickly as possible with a few quiet thanks and apologies to anyone who may need to move to let you pass.

During the performance

Every member of the audience should consider it his or her duty to inconvenience and disturb the rest of the audience as little as possible. Remember that you are only one of possibly hundreds of people who are there to enjoy the performance. You should make every effort to be quiet and still: constant rustling, talking and fidgeting can be very annoying and distracting for those around you.

It is also important not to do anything that might distract the performers. For this reason the use of flash photography is strictly forbidden in most auditoria. Not only can it annoy the rest of the audience it may break the concentration of the performers which might disrupt the scene or, in the case of ballet and other dance routines, could even be dangerous.

You should not leave your seat during a performance unless you absolutely have to, for example if you have a coughing fit or feel faint. If you need to cough once or twice it is better to let yourself cough than to try and smother the cough; the latter would only aggravate the tickle in your throat, probably making you cough more. Sneezes can usually be silenced by pinching the nose firmly as you sneeze.

If someone else in the audience is distracting you with repeated fidgeting or talking, try to catch their eye or tap them gently on the shoulder to let them know that they are inconveniencing you. Try not to say anything to him or her as this may provoke a loud retort; and certainly don't resort to saying 'sh' loudly as this will disturb the rest of the audience who may well have been oblivious to the original troublemaker.

Showing your appreciation

Applauding alone can be very embarrassing, so check before you put your hands together enthusiastically that you are doing so at the right moment. For most performances which include orchestras (such as concerts, operas, ballets and musicals) the audience will clap when the conductor enters the auditorium and, where applicable, when the soloist or first violinist arrives. If the set for a production is particularly beautiful or innovative the audience may clap as the curtains open.

In most productions the lighting will change or the curtains will come down to mark the end of scenes or acts, and these moments call for applause as does, of course, the end of the performance. In concerts, however, you should not clap between movements. Unless you are confident that you know the right moment to clap you should wait until the applause has already started.

In the theatre spontaneous applause during a performance, for example at the entrance of a famous actor or after the delivery of a well-known passage, is not usually acceptable. It may distract the performers and irritate the rest of the audience, although it is more acceptable in musicals. It is, however, quite commonplace to applaud an especially famous aria in an opera or a particularly well executed sequence in a ballet. Such applause is often accompanied by cries of 'bravo!' for a male performer or 'brava!' for a woman.

THEATRE TRIPS – CHECKLIST

Important dos and don'ts

✓ **DO plan to arrive in good time, especially if meeting people**
✓ **DO thank people if you disturb them to get to your seat**
✗ **DON'T talk or make a noise during the performance**
✗ **DON'T applaud at the wrong moments**

If you are so moved by something that you rise to your feet while clapping, have the courage of your convictions and others will usually join you by rising to their feet. You should sit back down again as the clapping subsides. Particularly well received productions or sequences may cause the audience to show their appreciation with enthusiastic slow handclapping, or to call 'encore!' in the hopes that the sequence will be repeated.

At the end of a musical performance of any kind you should not begin clapping until after the music has stopped: the orchestra is an integral part of the production. You should also remain in your seat until after the last curtain call; it is very disheartening for performers to see the audience sneaking away as they take their bows. During the final applause at first night performances there may be calls of 'author' and/or 'director'.

TRAVELLING ETIQUETTE

Many people spend a good proportion of their time travelling on public transport. Whether such travel forms part of a daily trip to work or a long-awaited annual holiday, it is made far more agreeable if people are polite and considerate towards their fellow travellers.

They should also respect the staff and regulations of the company with whom they are travelling: if there is a limitation on luggage you should respect it, or if you know that you are over the limit you should ring the company in advance to warn them and check the charges for excess baggage. You should also contact the company in advance if you have any kind of special needs: if, for example, you are disabled and will need assistance getting onto the means of transport; or if, on a service which provides meals, you have special dietary needs.

Queuing for tickets

The British are sometimes teased by other nations for their willingness to queue, but this willingness should not be mocked. However, queuing can be very frustrating especially if you are running late and if, as always seems to be the case, you feel you are in the slowest moving queue. But remember that everyone in the line is in the same situation as yourself and tolerate it with as good grace as you can manage.

Don't cramp the person immediately in front of you by edging your way closer and closer to them in the misguided belief that this will make the queue move more quickly. You will achieve little by sighing and tutting to show your impatience either with those ahead of you in the queue, or with the unfortunate person behind the counter who is trying to work under pressure. If you do demonstrate your impatience you will either fluster them, therefore making them less efficient, or annoy them so that they feel inclined to work slowly deliberately!

Finding a seat

On most forms of transport seats are not allocated, so you will have to find one. If there are no seats available and someone has put his or her luggage on a seat, ask politely if he or she could move the luggage so that you can sit down – no-one pays for bags to sit down! The personnel may be able to tell you where there are seats if you can't find any in the particular part of the train, bus or boat in which you are looking.

When you do find a seat say 'excuse me' and 'thank-you' to anyone who has to stand or move belongings for you to get to it. If someone offers you his or her seat, you should accept it with profuse thanks unless you really feel you do not need it, or you are only going a short distance, in which case you should still thank him or her and explain tactfully that you are quite happy to stand.

When you have a reserved seat, finding it should not be a problem but you can always ask for help from conductors, guards or other personnel. Should you find that someone is sitting in your reserved seat ask politely to see his or her ticket or reservation. If the person refuses to move from your seat, don't cause a scene, just get hold of a member of staff to sort out the problem. Obviously, if you find that you have inadvertently taken a reserved seat you should apologize and move immediately when the person holding the reservation arrives.

Once you have established where you are sitting, you should stow your luggage tidily so that it is neither taking up badly

needed seats nor blocking the gangways. Luggage stowed overhead should be secure so that it is not likely to fall down and
injure anyone.

Do give up your seat if there is someone who needs it more
than you: the elderly, the disabled, pregnant women or women
trying to cope with small children should all be given priority. If
you want to offer your seat to someone stand up, move aside and
then say 'would you like my seat?'. If you are already on your feet
your offer looks far more genuine than if you are still comfortably ensconced. If you are sitting next to an empty seat
it is also polite and thoughtful to move to a single seat in order
to free the double space for two people who are travelling
together.

During the journey

During the course of your journey you should make sure that
you don't inconvenience other passengers. Don't talk too
loudly, play loud music or listen to a very noisy personal stereo;
don't spread yourself, your belongings or the newspaper you are
reading at the expense of fellow travellers; don't throw litter;
and don't smoke in a no smoking area.

Apologize if cramped conditions mean that you occasionally
nudge your neighbours in the ribs, and always ask those around
you before opening or closing windows. Help other people if
they are having trouble stowing their luggage or opening or closing a window. Finally, if you are travelling with children, make
sure that you have plenty of things to keep them occupied as well
as snacks and drinks to keep them happy.

If someone in the carriage is disturbing you or behaving
offensively, try to ask politely for him or her to stop. If this does
not succeed you would be better off moving to another seat or
contacting the personnel rather than provoking a scene.

SPECIAL OCCASIONS

Conductors, guards and other personnel

All travel company personnel should be treated with the courtesy and respect with which you would expect them to treat you. They should certainly not be blamed for delays or other problems for which they can't be held responsible. Most of the personnel who work on trains, buses and coaches are well informed and they should be able to tell you about timetables and connections. Make their jobs easier by having the fare ready for bus drivers or conductors, and tickets ready for inspection by train conductors. You should have bought a ticket before boarding a train, but if you did not have time to do so, go to the conductor immediately to buy one.

Coach tours

On a coach tour you will find yourself in close proximity with the same group of people for most of your holiday. You should, therefore, make every effort to be both tolerable and tolerant: don't do things that you know will annoy or inconvenience fellow travellers; on the other hand, try to put up with any behaviour of theirs that might irritate you. If something that someone is doing – such as smoking in the coach or talking loudly when others are trying to sleep – really annoys you, try talking to them about it tactfully rather than confronting them aggressively.

Coach tours usually work on tight schedules and every member of the group owes it to the other passengers to be punctual so that the schedule can be adhered to. Make sure that you are ready in time for the morning departure and always observe the rendezvous times given at the end of an excursion.

Air travel

As with all forms of travel, punctuality is very important when you are travelling by air. When an airline requires you to check in, for example, two hours before the flight, they do not mean within two hours prior to the departure time, but at least two hours prior to the departure time. This gives them time to carry out all the necessary security checks before passengers and baggage can board the plane. If you check in in good time you will also be more likely to have the seat of your choice during the flight. You should respect this time period and be tolerant of all security checks: they are there to protect your life.

Once you have checked in, make sure that you actually board the plane in good time; don't ignore the 'now boarding' and 'last call' signs on the departures board. For security reasons the plane can't take off without you once your luggage has been loaded onto the plane. If you are late you will delay the take-off, making yourself very unpopular with the crew and the other passengers; this is particularly true of charter flights which may be kept waiting for several hours for the next free take-off slot in a busy airport.

Your seat number will be marked on your boarding pass, and if you have any trouble finding it you should ask a member of the cabin staff to help you. If someone is sitting in your seat or if you seem to be sitting in someone else's seat, check the seat numbers on your boarding passes and, of course, apologize profusely if you were in the wrong.

When you find your seat, stow your luggage safely either under the seat in front of you or in the overhead lockers, as instructed by the cabin staff. Apologize to anyone who has to move for you to get to your seat, and make sure that you have everything that you are likely to need during the flight so that you don't disturb them too often as you go backwards and forwards to the overhead locker to get a magazine, a book, and then your knitting! If someone needs to get past you, always stand aside as promptly as possible. If they seem to get up very often and you are trying to sleep or concentrate on something, ask them whether they would mind changing places with you.

If you strike up a conversation with those next to you, check for signs that they might want to break up the conversation in order to sleep or read. If your neighbour insists on engaging you in a long conversation when you would rather be doing something else, let them know politely.

For the safety and comfort of other passengers you should observe the 'no smoking' signs and, even if you are sitting in a smoking area, you should check whether those around you mind before lighting a cigarette. Many airlines offer free drinks during the flight; however tempting it may be to make the most of this bounty, you should try to moderate your drinking for your own sake and for the sake of the other passengers. Altitude tends to exaggerate the effects of alcohol, so you may become a nuisance to fellow travellers. You are also more likely to feel ill under the effects of alcohol during a flight than under normal circumstances, especially as both alcohol and the cabin's air conditioning system are dehydrating.

TRAVELLING – CHECKLIST

Important dos and don'ts

✓ **DO show consideration and politeness to fellow travellers**
✓ **DO give up your seat to someone who needs it more**
✗ **DON'T take up more than you fair share of space**

VISITING THE SICK

When people are ill they usually derive a great deal of pleasure from a visit. Much of their time is spent alone and possibly bored and/or in discomfort; a visit from someone and the gift of conversation with him or her should cheer them up and break up the monotony of their day. Don't shy away from visiting someone in hospital or ill at home – especially if he or she has asked you to drop in; your visit need only be brief and, however anxious you may be about it, you can be sure that it will give pleasure.

Should you visit?

If someone that you know is very ill and you would like to visit him or her, it is often best to check first whether a visit would be suitable. Ask a close friend or relation or, if he or she is in hospital, check with the hospital staff. They will be able to tell you whether or not the patient is receiving visitors. They may also warn you if, for example, you should not expect much in the way of response from the patient. Even those who are unconscious or unable to communicate may draw great strength from your visit, and the stimulation may even help their recovery.

Timing your visit

Before visiting someone who is sick you should check the hospital's visiting hours or, if the patient is at home, check with his or her family when it would be convenient for you to drop in. Hospitals may also restrict the number of people who can be with the patient at any one time, so be patient and wait your time within the allotted visiting hours. It goes without saying that close family and friends should be given precedence at the patient's bedside.

When you are with the patient keep an eye on the way he or she responds to you. Be sensitive to the fact that the sick often find it difficult to concentrate for any length of time, and leave when you feel your friend is becoming tired. On the other hand if he or she is obviously craving company and conversation stay on as long as you can.

Taking things

It is customary to take small gifts when visiting the sick. Traditionally visitors take flowers or fruit, but magazines or books might be more practical. Check with the patient's close family and friends or with the hospital to see if there is something that would really give him or her pleasure. If you know you will be visiting several times ask the patient in person if there is something he or she would particularly like you to bring the next time. If he or she asks for food or drink, you should always check with the hospital staff whether this would be compatible with their treatment. Cigarettes and alcohol are completely banned in most hospitals.

Making conversation

Many people avoid visiting friends in hospital because they are not sure what to say or talk about; they may feel awkward in the presence of another person's obvious pain or discomfort. All these considerations should be brushed aside – what is important to the patient is that you have made the effort to go and see him or her.

It is almost inevitable that the conversation will begin with the visitor asking 'how are you?', but it is best if the conversation does not dwell on the details of the patient's condition; that is, of course, unless he or she seems to want to talk about it. What the patient probably wants to hear about is the outside world, so tell him or her what you have been doing, and this should spark off questions and a natural conversation.

VISITING THE SICK – CHECKLIST

Important dos and don'ts

✓ **DO make the effort to visit sick friends, it is appreciated**
✓ **DO check first what times are convenient**
✓ **DO ask if there is anything that they need**
✗ **DON'T stay if the patient appears to be getting tired**

WEDDINGS

A wedding is not only meant to be one of the happiest days in a person's life it may also be one of the most stressful. A large wedding will take considerable time to organize, so all parties need to be prepared for these difficulties and should be ready to make compromises.

Once the legal formalities (detailed below) have been satisfied, the couple can start planning the wedding: what kind of marriage ceremony do they want? when and where will they hold the reception? how many guests will they invite? Answering these questions is just the beginning, the actual work involved in preparing a full church wedding with a large reception will probably take at least three months.

Legal requirements

The minimum legal age for marriage is 16. In England and Wales anyone between the ages of 16 and 18 must have the written consent of their parents or guardians, however, such consent is not required in Scotland. There are also civil and religious laws concerning the marrying of blood relations and relations by marriage; if in doubt, ask a priest or registrar about the forbidden categories. Divorced people are forbidden from remarrying until the decree absolute has come through.

Except in Scotland, the marriage ceremony must be held in a registered place of worship or a registrar office (except for Jewish and Quaker weddings, which may, by leave of a special licence, be held wherever they choose), and in an area where either or both of the couple live. The ceremony must be legally recognized whether religious or civil, according to the rites of the Church of England, or the rites of another religious denomination with a certificate issued by the civil superintendent registrar of marriages, or a civil ceremony held in a register office conducted by a registrar of marriages. Whatever the ceremony it has to be performed between 8 am and 6 pm.

The marriage must be witnessed by a minimum of two people over the age of 18, and by a person authorized to conduct the service.

Religious and civil weddings

Whether civil or religious, in a church or registry office, there are various requirements and stipulations that have to be met before a ceremony can take place.

Church of England

A marriage may be performed by the Church of England in three ways: by publication of the banns; by common licence; by special licence. The Church of England requires that at least one of the couple must have been baptized into the Christian church, and a divorced person will not be married if their former spouse is still alive. It is usual for the marriage to take place in the bride's church, but it may be held in any church if either or both of their names are on the electoral register of that parish, or if one of them establishes residence in the parish of the chosen church for 15 days prior to the ceremony.

Marriage by banns

The vicar reads out the banns in church on three successive Sundays. The purpose is to allow anyone who may know of reasons why the marriage should not take place to object. If the groom is from another parish he must inform his vicar of the proposed marriage. His vicar will then arrange with the bride's vicar that the banns are read in both churches on the same three Sundays. The groom's vicar will then provide a certificate stating that he has read the banns – without this certificate the wedding cannot take place.

Once the banns have been read the marriage may take place at any time within the following three months. However, if the marriage does not take place within this period the banns must be read again.

Marriage by common licence

A common licence may be sought when a couple cannot wait the required 21 days it takes to read the banns. The couple apply for the licence through their clergyman, with the approval of the local diocesan council. One of the couple must be resident in the parish for at least 15 days before the wedding.

A common licence is required when one or both of the couple is not a British citizen or are not resident in England and Wales.

Once the licence is issued the wedding may take place with only one day's notice, and it is valid for three months.

Marriage by special licence

A special licence is issued for exceptional circumstances, such as the bride or groom being too ill to marry in a church. This licence allows for a marriage to be held at any time and in any place, such as a private chapel, a hospital or any place not authorized for marriage ceremonies. It can only be issued with the approval of the Archbishop of Canterbury.

Church of Scotland

A couple may be married in any church or place of their choosing, and there are no residential requirements to be met. The Church of Scotland does not require the reading of banns, but the couple must submit a notice of marriage to the civil registrar 4 weeks (6 if previously married) before the date, and a Schedule of Marriage will then be issued if the registrar is satisfied. The notice must be signed in front of two witnesses, who must be householders, and who also sign. The notice is then put on view at the registrar's office, of the district in which the couple live, for seven days to allow for anyone to come forward with an objection to the marriage. Once a Schedule is issued it is valid for three months.

The Schedule must be signed after the ceremony by the couple, the minister and two witnesses (over 14), and returned within three days to the registrar.

The Roman Catholic Church

For a Roman Catholic marriage a couple will have to obtain a certificate from their superintendent registrar (see civil weddings, below).

The couple's priest will usually require two or three days to discuss the marriage with them and to complete all the paperwork. The couple must provide their baptism and confirmation certificates before the priest can fill in their pre-nuptial enquiry forms. If the bride or groom is not marrying in his or her parish church, permission must be given and a letter of freedom provided. The banns will only be read if both are Catholics.

For a Catholic to marry a non-Catholic, and if the ceremony is to take place in a church of another denomination, a dispensation must be granted.

Nonconformists

As for Roman Catholic weddings, a marriage performed by a Nonconformist church (that is outside the established Church of England) requires a certificate from the superintendent registrar (see below). Also, it may be that the particular sect is too small to have a minister authorized to perform a marriage ceremony, in which case a registrar will have to be present. The registrar will not conduct the ceremony, but registers that it has taken place.

Jewish weddings

As for Nonconformists notice of the wedding must be made to the local superintendent registrar. However, Jewish weddings may be held wherever the couple choose, for instance, a private house, and in most cases the registrar will not need to attend because the secretary of the synagogue will be authorized to register a wedding.

Hindu, Muslim and Sikh weddings

The couple married according to one of these faiths must legalize their marriage in a civil ceremony, either before or after the religious ceremony.

Civil weddings

There are certain legal requirements which must be satisfied before a couple may marry in a register office. It is important to note that (as with religious ceremonies) the requirements for civil weddings in England and Wales are not the same as those in Scotland.

Superintendent registrar's certificate

A couple may marry in any register office, but they must have been resident in the particular office's district for a minimum of seven days. The superintendent registrar will require documented proof that the couple are of legal age, and if either had been previously married proof of divorce or a death certificate. The documents must be the actual ones, photocopies are not acceptable. If these requirements are met the registrar will then display a notice of marriage for 21 days (there is a fee for this notice). If the bride and groom live in different districts notice must be given to the registrar in both districts. After the 21 days, and no objection to the marriage has been made, a certificate is issued to either of the couple in person. The marriage can then take place, in a building registered for wedding ceremonies, at any time within three months from the date that notice of the wedding was entered by the registrar.

This certificate is also required for any wedding that is not performed by the Church of England.

Superintendent registrar's licence

Such a licence may be sought when a couple, for whatever reason, needs to marry quickly and wishes to avoid the 21 days notice of the wedding.

Either one of the couple must have been a resident in the register office's district for at least 15 days. The marriage must take place in the district that the licence is granted, in a building registered for weddings, and there must be one day between the issue of the licence and the wedding. The couple may then marry within three months from the date of application.

Scotland

There is no residential qualification, but 15 days' notice must be given prior to the date of the wedding. If the bride or groom is a resident of Wales or England a superintendent registrar's certificate is acceptable, and must be applied for in the usual way (see above). The couple must sign a notice of marriage in front of two householders, who must also sign the document. If the registrar is satisfied with the notice, it is then put on view for seven days. After this period, and if no objections have been made, a certificate of publication is issued and the couple may marry at any time within the next three months.

SPECIAL OCCASIONS

Planning the wedding service

If the wedding is to be held in a church, the chosen church will have to be booked well in advance, and the couple may have to alter the preferred date or time of their wedding to fit in with existing bookings. The vicar or priest may want to talk to both partners about the state of matrimony in the eyes of God. He will certainly want to discuss the order of service, and he may be able to suggest suitable readings, hymns and pieces of music. The order of service can vary considerably: in most wedding services the actual marriage takes place near the beginning of the service, but it may occur at any time as may a reading and/or an address, and prayers, all punctuated by hymns.

The vicar's fees should also be discussed at this stage; these are traditionally borne by the groom. If you would like a different vicar to take all or part of the service you should introduce this idea tactfully. For his part, the vicar will let you know if for any reason photography and video recording is not permitted in the church and he may ask if you would mind him forbidding the use of confetti in or outside the church.

You can also talk to the vicar about the choir, organist and bell-ringers if you are planning to use them on the day. He should be able to tell you how to book them and what their fees are likely to be. There may be a local flower guild or a flower rota for decorating the church, and he will be able to put you in touch with them to arrange the flowers for the wedding day (if there is more than one wedding on that day, you will have to contact the other couple to discuss colour schemes!) If you are planning a large guest list, you should also check with the vicar how many people the church can seat.

For a register office wedding plan well in advance, especially to make sure that they can book the register office for the date that suits them. They should check how many people the register office will hold before inviting too many friends; then they can send out printed or hand-written invitations.

The ceremony may be a quiet affair or it may be to all intents and purposes like a church wedding with a white dress, brides-maids and guests in hats with confetti. In any event it will be short: the registrar will first talk to the couple alone and settle the fee with them, before conducting the 10-minute ceremony.

Important planning guidelines

There are so many things that need to be organized for a big wedding that it is easy to forget an important detail until it is too late. This little section – although not definitive – covers most of the elements that need to be dealt with in advance.

It goes without saying that you will have to book a church or register office, but do it in plenty of time to ensure you get the date you prefer. You may also want to hire the service of bell-ringers, a choir, an organist, a soloist or other musicians, and if you plan to marry during the height of the 'wedding season' these people are probably booked-up well in advance.

You may need to hire a venue or marquee for the reception; if you have marquee it may need tables, chairs, flooring, lining, heating and lighting. You will probably have to employ caterers, and possibly a separate cake-maker. If there is to be a sit-down meal at the reception, you will have to devise a seating plan. You may want to hire a band or a disco.

You will also have to draw up a guest list, and possibly a list of wedding presents, and you may want to have invitations and service sheets printed.

The flowers will need to be arranged in advance: flowers in the church and at the reception as well as the bride's bouquet, posies for bridesmaids and buttonholes for the groom, best man and ushers. If the bride is to have fresh flowers in her hair, she will need to discuss this with the florist and her hairdresser. She may anyway want to make an appointment with her hairdresser and a make-up expert for the morning of the wedding. Even when the bouquets are booked you have to be sure that you know who is picking them up and when, and how they are being paid for.

The bride's dress is hardly likely to be forgotten, but if the dress is to be made the bride should allow plenty of time so that it is ready before the wedding, but she should have a final fitting within a week of the wedding in case she has gained or lost weight. The bride will also need to buy a going away outfit. The bridesmaid's dresses are traditionally paid for by the bridesmaid's themselves or, if they are very young, by their parents. If this is the case, the bride should introduce the idea to them tactfully and should try to make sure that the dresses will be of some practical use to them after the wedding.

The groom may need to hire his clothes, and this should be done in good time to make sure that he has a suit and all the trimmings to fit him well. He may also want his best man and male relations to be fitted out by the same hire company.

Most couples like to have a photographer and many choose to have their wedding recorded on video or audio tape. They should check with the vicar whether photographing and filming are allowed in the church. They should also try to speak to several different photographers and, if possible look at their portfolios. When they have quotes from a number of different photographers they can choose the one that suits their needs best.

Cars may have to be booked to take the bride and her family, and the groom and best man, to the church; to take the bridal party from the church to the reception; and to take the newly married couple away at the end of the reception. You should also think a little bit about where your guests are going to park during the service and the reception, and how they are to get from one to the other. If you have invited a large number of guests, you may want to warn the local police station, who may allow you to reserve certain parking spaces.

Some people like to hire a Master of Ceremonies to announce guests as they arrive at the reception; to announce the speakers during the speeches; and to generally stage manage the reception. Some even lay on a crèche facility during the service and/or the reception. Finally, if you would like a newspaper announcement to appear after the wedding, it is usually best to have the wording worked out in advance; you can check the usual format in the newspaper you have chosen.

Wedding presents

Many couples choose to draw up a wedding list to help their guests choose presents for them. Although all the guests who attend a wedding should bring a gift, it is considered rude to send out information about the wedding list with invitations. Some guests don't like the idea of wedding lists and prefer to choose a gift without any guidance, but there is no denying that wedding lists are a practical idea. They are the best way of ensuring that the newly weds have everything they need to set up their new life, and of minimizing the embarrassing incidence of duplicated presents. Couples using the wedding list system should make sure that their chosen gifts cover a wide range of different prices.

The easiest way to arrange your wedding list is to have the entire list at one store. Stores that run this service will tell you how to draw up your list; you will probably be given forms to fill to show how many of which items you would like. If guests call you to find out what you would like as a wedding present you can put them in touch with the shop, but it is best to provide the name and telephone number of the store on the list. They should be able to deal directly with the shop's wedding list service, either by visiting the shop in person or by buying the gift over the telephone by credit card. Many shops will arrange to store goods until after the wedding, or to deliver each gift as it is ordered.

Some couples prefer more freedom than this, and they compile a list of things that they would like from any number of different shops. They then make a few copies of this list and send it to those who ask for it. They may even write their list of presents in spiral bound notebooks, so that each guest tears out the page on which the gift they have chosen appears before sending it on to another guest or returning it to the engaged couple.

The most important thing to remember about wedding presents is that you should always write a letter of thanks. If you receive presents before the wedding, try to write and thank immediately; you may be inundated with gifts at the wedding and will wish you had got as many letters written as possible before the wedding.

The guest list

The factors limiting your guest list will probably be your budget and the size of either your church or your reception venue. If you are to be married in a very small church it is perfectly acceptable to invite only immediate family and very close friends to the service and to ask the bulk of your guests to the reception afterwards. Conversely, if the service is to be held in a large church but you can't afford a big reception you can invite most of the guests to the service and only add the words '.. and afterwards at the Black Swan Hotel', for example, on a few of the invitations. If an afternoon reception is turning into a dancing party in the evening, it is quite normal to expect certain guests to leave at the end of the afternoon when the couple retire to change, and to invite a further group of friends to join the party in the evening.

It is best to decide a ceiling for the number of guests that you can invite before writing down a single name – this makes it easier to be ruthless with numbers if you need to be. Traditionally, the entire guest list was drawn up by the bride's parents. Nowadays they will tend to give the groom's parents and the couple themselves a 'quota' of guests – this should be the case if the cost of the reception is to be shared. Even so, as the bride's parents are still technically the host of the reception and their names appear on the invitations, they may like to send out all the invitations themselves. They should, therefore, be given the names and addresses of guests to be invited by the other parties.

When compiling guest lists remember that only two-thirds to three-quarters of those invited will actually accept the invitation, so you can afford to invite more than your maximum capacity. If you are having to be strict on numbers remember that family and lasting friends should have priority. You are under no obligation to invite the boyfriends or girlfriends of your friends, especially if you have not met them; but it is rude to ask a married or engaged person without asking his or her partner.

In general it is considered rude or unfair to ask two people who do not like each other (great business rivals or a couple who have undergone an acrimonious divorce) to the same occasion. With weddings, however, you can usually get away with it. It is your day and, if you would particularly like both parties to attend, they should be able to avoid each other – or even bury the hatchet – for the duration of one day. On the other hand, the bride and groom should be wary of inviting too many of their own ex-boyfriends and ex-girlfriends respectively. Unless your partner has had an opportunity to meet or at least talk about your past conquests, having them paraded before him or her on such an important day may be intolerable.

SPECIAL OCCASIONS

Invitations

Wedding invitations are usually printed on stiff card folded once
to about the size of a paperback book. There are, however,
countless different formats and forms of wording; most printers
or stationers will let you choose from catalogues.

Traditionally, wedding invitations come from the bride's
mother. Couples who are remarrying, however, tend to send out
invitations in their own names, for example, 'Matthew and
Elizabeth request the pleasure of your company . . . etc.' The
wording on a traditional formal wedding invitation reads as follows:

Mr and Mrs Philip Tremaine
request the pleasure of your company
at the marriage of their daughter
Anita Jane
to
Mr Arthur Carver
at St Mary's Church, Stockbridge
on Saturday 29th July
at 12 noon
and afterwards at
The Star Hotel, Stockbridge

The letters RSVP and the address to which replies should be
sent usually appear in the bottom left-hand corner. Guests'
names, for example, 'Dr and Mrs Patrick Williams', should be
handwritten in the top left-hand corner of the invitation.

If the bride's parents are divorced they will usually put their
names separately, for example, 'Mr Philip Tremaine and Mrs
Melissa Tremaine'. If the mother has remarried, the invitation
may still come from the bride's two parents, but they will usually
put their names on separate lines, for example:

Mr Philip Tremaine
and Mrs Melissa Marshall

If the invitation comes from the bride's mother and stepfather, their surname will not be the same as the bride's, and it may be worthwhile including her surname on the invitation, for example:

Mr and Mrs Roger Marshall
request the pleasure of your company
at the marriage of her daughter
Anita Jane Tremaine

In this way guests don't have trouble working out whose wedding they have been invited to!

Wedding invitations are usually sent out about six weeks in advance. You will, therefore, need to get in touch with the printer some two to three months prior to the wedding in order to allow time for choosing a style, reading the proofs and the printing process itself.

Planning the reception

The wedding reception is traditionally arranged by the bride's parents and held at their home. But, of course, it can be held anyway that the couple choose, in an hotel, a restaurant or village hall, even a river boat, private house, park or place of historic interest. If the reception is to be held outside you will probably need to hire a marquee in case it rains.

Whichever location you choose, you will probably have to bear in mind the hire fees and you will certainly have to book it some time in advance; particularly if you plan to marry in the late spring, early summer, which is the most popular time for weddings. You should also check how practical it will be for the caterers, for the number of guests you are planning and for guest parking.

The type of catering that a family chooses to have for a wedding reception depends on their budget and on the time of day of the service. A morning or midday service should be followed by a buffet or sit-down lunch, and the couple will usually leave towards 4 or 5 pm. Weddings held in the early afternoon are usually followed by a stand-up reception at which canapés are served; tea and sweetmeats are usually served later in the afternoon, and the couple will leave at about 7 pm unless the reception is continuing into the evening. After a late afternoon service, the reception should include a buffet or sit-down dinner, possibly with dancing after the meal, and the couple should leave not later than midnight.

Whatever food is served at the wedding it is customary to serve champagne to drink. It is of course perfectly acceptable to serve a sparkling white wine or any other kind of drink, but soft drinks should always be available as an alternative. Some families serve the drink of their choice for most of the reception and bring out the champagne for the toasts. In any event the caterers should be told when the speeches and toasts are about to be made so that they can make a point of topping up all the guests' glasses.

It is very difficult for the family themselves to provide the catering for a wedding; this will really only work for a very small reception or a particularly organized family who have few arguments! If the family does undertake the catering they will find it very draining before, during and after the wedding day, which really should be a time of happiness and celebration.

Most people will decide to use caterers. The names of local firms can be found in yellow pages; the managers of the venue hired for the reception may have their own caterers, or they may be able to recommend a catering service. It is best to discuss your requirements with several companies and to get quotes from all of them before deciding which to use.

Paying for a wedding

As the wedding and the reception are traditionally arranged by the bride's parents and the guest list drawn up by them, it is also traditionally their responsibility to pay for the day and almost everything it entails. This includes the hire of a venue, of caterers, the purchase of drink, the hire of cars to the church and the purchase of the bride's dress, among other things.

The groom is then held responsible for paying for the church fees; the wedding ring; the bride's bouquet; buttonholes for himself, his best man and the ushers; transport from the church to the reception; gifts for the attendants; and transport to leave at the end of the reception.

These strict codes are no longer obeyed so closely; it is now perfectly acceptable and even expected for the couple them-selves or the groom's parents either to organize the reception, to pay for it or to contribute in some way to the final bill. Even if the bride's parents are quite happy to pay for the entire reception, the groom's parents may like to offer to contribute something specific, such as the purchase of the champagne or the hire of musicians.

The best man

The role of the best man during the build up to a wedding and on the day itself is an extremely important one. Firstly – in chrono-logical order rather than order of importance – the best man is usually responsible for organizing the groom's stag party. He must also liaise with the groom prior to the wedding in order to ensure that he knows exactly what he will be expected to do on the day.

SPECIAL OCCASIONS

His chief duties on the day of the wedding are to make sure that the groom gets to the church on time – and in a fit state; to look after the ring until the moment during the service when it is needed; and to make a speech during the reception. He may be required to pay all the fees at the church on behalf of the groom. He may also be needed as a general usher and stage manager, making sure that all the right people are in the right place at the right time for the photographs, the speeches, the cutting of the cake and the departure of the bride and groom. He is often privy to secret information about where the couple will be spending their first night and their honeymoon, so that he can help to arrange transport there and can ensure that their luggage is in the car waiting for them when they leave.

For obvious reasons the best man should be a close friend of the groom. Traditionally, he was a bachelor, though it is now perfectly acceptable for the best man to be married. The groom should think carefully before choosing his best man: he will need someone reliable, organized, possibly discreet and preferably imaginative and humorous enough to deal cheerfully with problems and to make an entertaining speech.

Attendants

The bride may be attended by any number of bridesmaids, pageboys and flower girls. It is up to the bride to choose them and to decide what they should wear, but – as the cost of their clothes is usually borne by themselves or their families – she should give them some say in what they wear. It is usual for at least one member of the bridal party to come from the groom's family.

The main function of bridesmaids and pageboys is to look decorous and, if the bride has a very long train and/or veil, to carry these as the bride advances along the aisle. Flower girls carry bouquets, hoops or balls of flowers. Bridesmaids can be of any age, although the very young may be more disruptive than enchanting. Married women may also attend the bride; they are known as matrons of honour.

Amongst the bride's attendants there should be one brides-maid – usually the oldest, or a close friend or relation of the bride – who will be the chief bridesmaid, and she has several duties to fulfil. She is usually expected to help the bride dress and to keep her calm immediately before leaving the house to go to the church. Before, during and after the service she should keep all the younger attendants under control and make sure that they know what they are meant to be doing. During the service she will take the bride's bouquet and she may help the bride to lift her veil at the relevant moment; if the bride is to give the groom a ring, this may be entrusted to the chief bridesmaid until it is needed in the service.

The bride should ask those she would like to be her attendants (and, if they are young, their parents) well in advance and, to avoid embarrassment later, should make it clear who will be paying for their outfits. She should also help the groom to buy a little gift of thanks for each of her attendants; these will be given to them during the reception, possibly during the bridegroom's speech.

Ushers

In a big church wedding it may be necessary to have ushers to distribute service sheets, to ensure that the correct number of pews are reserved for the immediate families of the bride and groom, and to show guests to their seats. Those who are chosen as ushers should ideally know some relations and friends of the bride and/or groom. If an usher does not recognize a guest, he should ask 'bride or groom?': guests who are friends of the bride should be seated to the left of the aisle as one looks at the altar, and friends of the groom to the right.

SPECIAL OCCASIONS

A rehearsal

It is often a good idea to have a rehearsal for a church wedding. This will help if anyone involved in the ceremony is very nervous or if the attendants are very young and need to be shown what to do during the service. The time of the rehearsal should be arranged with the vicar; the most convenient time is usually the evening before the wedding when many of the dramatis personnae will already be in the area.

The minister will talk everyone through the key parts of the service, and will give the bride and her father an opportunity to practice walking up the aisle at a sedate pace, possibly with the relevant music playing. He should also check that the bride's father, the bride and the groom understand how the bride's hand is transferred from her father to the groom at the moment when she is given away. He may ask the couple to practice the exchange of rings.

The vicar will also discuss with the couple whether they would like to remain at the altar rail for the entire service or whether they would like to sit in the pews, for example during the address if there is to be one. Some vicars like the couple to move up to the altar during the prayers. Finally, he will show the wedding party how to get to the vestry for the signing of the register and he will allow the bride and groom, and their attendants, to practice walking back down the aisle.

On the day – the service

The ushers may need to be at the church about half an hour before the service is due to begin in order to sort out service sheets and to check that the front pews on both sides of the church have been reserved for the bride and groom's immediate families. The best man should get the groom to the church with about 10 minutes to spare, and they should take up their places in the front right hand pew until the bride arrives.

The bride should be preceded to the church by her mother and her attendants. She should be last to arrive with her father or whoever is giving her away (this may be her stepfather, godfather, brother or even a female relation). If the bride is to be given away by her father or stepfather the family should ensure that another man, possibly a brother, escorts her mother to the church and to her seat in the front left hand pew.

The bride, her father and attendants should progress slowly up the aisle with the bride on her father's right arm. At this stage the groom should be waiting for her at the altar rail and turning to watch her arrive; his best man should be just to his right.

During the actual marriage ceremony the bride and groom should say their vows slowly and clearly. If they are very nervous they should watch the vicar closely: he probably performs marriages at least once a week in the summer, and he will guide them through, even telling them when to say 'I will' if they seem to have forgotten.

During the signing of the register the bride and her attendants should take the opportunity to straighten headdresses and to sort out the train in preparation for the triumphant exit of the newly married couple. The bride and groom will lead the procession, with the bride on the groom's left arm. They will be followed by their attendants and then by their parents: the mother of the bride with the father of the groom, and the mother of the groom with the father of the bride.

The couple may want their photographer to take a number of photographs outside the church; photographs of different family groups can take a long time to organize so the best man and even some of the ushers should be enlisted to make sure that everyone is available when they are needed. As soon as the photographs are over the wedding party should be driven away to the reception so that they have a moment to catch their breath before the first guests arrive.

SPECIAL OCCASIONS

On the day – the reception

Many families choose to have a receiving line to welcome guests to the wedding. Although this may cause considerable queuing time for the guests, it is the best way of ensuring that the wedding party actually greets every guest. The receiving line is usually organized so that the guests are greeted by the wedding party in the following order: the mother of the bride, the father of the bride, the mother of the groom, the father of the groom, the bride and then the groom.

If the reception is particularly large, the waiting time may be reduced by having only the bride and groom in the receiving line. While guests are waiting to be received caterers should ensure that they are served with drinks, and ushers may be able to relieve them of coats and last-minute presents.

Once the last guests have arrived the wedding party may be involved in another photographic session. Then the reception proper can begin with the bride and groom circulating amongst their guest and trying to talk to as many of them as possible. If a meal is to be served it should be served at this stage in the proceedings, and if a seating plan is being used it should have been displayed where all the guests will have had a chance to see it. The top table should be reserved for the immediate wedding party. If the vicar is attending the reception he should also be seated at the top table and he should be invited to say grace before the meal begins.

After the meal, or at a prearranged time during a reception that does not include a meal, the best man or master of ceremonies should call for silence so that the father of the bride can make his speech. Although the first speech is traditionally made by the father of the bride, a close friend of the bride's family is equally suitable.

The object of the first speech is to tell the listeners, especially those who don't know the bride, something about the bride. The layout of the speech can be based on the pattern described above, and the two or three points may be about particular characteristics of the bride, which can be illustrated by anecdotes from her past. The father-of-the-bride speech ends with a toast to the bride and groom.

It is then the turn of the groom to respond to the toast by thanking the first speaker on behalf of his new wife and himself. The groom then makes a brief speech in which he must remember to thank his parents-in-law for their daughter, and to thank all those who have contributed to the smooth running of the wedding day. This speech can turn into a monotonous list of thank-yous if the groom does not make an effort to introduce a few humorous and touching details about the work that has gone into making the day a success. The groom should end his speech by thanking the attendants (matron of honour, bridesmaids, pageboys and/or flower girls) and by proposing a toast to them.

The best man then responds to this toast on behalf of the attendants, thanking the groom for his words about them. He then speaks about the groom for the sake of those who do not know him, and usually much to the amusement of those who do. The best man's speech is often the most entertaining (because it is easier and more acceptable to make jokes at the expense of the groom than of the bride). But the best man should bear in mind that he may be speaking to mixed company of mixed ages, and he should moderate his humour accordingly.

During his speech the best man may read out a few cards and telegrams from close friends and relations of the bride and groom who have not been able to attend on the day. He usually ends his speech by proposing a second toast to the bride and groom.

The cutting of the cake usually follows the speeches. Once the cake has been ceremoniously cut the bride and groom are free to circulate again, and the caterers can take the cake away to cut it up and distribute it to guests. Depending on the time of day, it may be suitable to serve tea and/or coffee with the cake. Some couples like to save the top tier of their wedding cake as a christening cake for the first child, and many families like to package little portions of the cake and post them to friends and relations who were not able to attend the wedding.

The best man will have been told at what time the bride and groom are planning to leave and he should warn them when this time is approaching so that they can go and change. The chief bridesmaid should help the bride change into her going away outfit and should make sure that her wedding dress is hung up carefully and that her luggage for the honeymoon is in the car that she will be leaving in. She should also make sure that the bride still has her bouquet with her.

The groom should also go to change and should collect his bride when she is ready to leave. The bride and groom should each say goodbye to their own parents and to their newly acquired parents-in-law. Finally, before being driven away, the bride should throw her bouquet into the crowd: it is said that the girl who catches it will be the next to marry.

Being a wedding guest

If you are invited to a wedding you should reply to the invitation as soon as possible whether or not you can attend. You should also look into the question of a wedding present; every guest should give the bride and groom a present. Whether or not you choose to buy a gift of your choice or one from the couple's wedding list, it is best to get it as soon as possible. This will give the couple more time to write you a thank-you letter. If you do take a present on the day, make sure that it is clearly labelled and don't try to hand it directly to the couple, but find out where they have arranged for presents to be left.

You should always make every effort to arrive in good time so that you can park and find a good place in the church. At most weddings men wear either morning suits or lounge suits, with women in correspondingly smart clothes including hats and gloves if they wish. If you have children but their names are not included on the invitation, you should assume that they have not been invited. In any event, you should check with the family before taking children or babies to a wedding. You should keep them quiet and under control during the service and the reception, and should take them out immediately if they threaten to spoil the service.

The guests' main duty during the reception is to enjoy themselves. They should circulate and should make sure they do not drink too much; they should temper any colourful remarks they may be tempted to make during the speeches and they should not hold the bride and groom in conversation for too long.

Guests should leave very shortly after the bride and groom have left, and they should make a point of thanking the bride's parents before they leave. Although it is not necessary to write a letter of thanks after a wedding reception, many people do, and these letters are warmly appreciated by all those who put so much effort into making the day a success.

A TO Z SECTION

addressing envelopes

Write the address about half way down towards the left-hand margin and always use the postcode if you know it. For letters or parcels being sent abroad put the letters 'Exp' (from the French word *expéditeur* – 'sender') followed by your own name and address on the back. Indeed, the Post Office recommend that the sender's name and address should be written on the back of any letter or parcel in case it goes to the wrong address or is undelivered for some reason.

When addressing a letter to a man use either Mr, his title or his rank. Some people use 'Esq.' after a man's name, as a sign of respect, for example, 'Edward Mallard, Esq.'. But 'Esq.' cannot be combined with Mr or any other title. If a person has honours, it is a sign of respect to add the letters after his or her name on an envelope.

Addressing letters to a woman is more difficult: a woman may be Miss, Mrs, Ms or she may have some form of title. Traditionally a married or widowed woman is addressed using her husband's name, for example Mrs John Carmichael; and a divorcée uses her own name, for example Mrs Sheila Carmichael. Many women now prefer to be addressed using their own name even if they are married, and some professional women still use their maiden names for business purposes even after they are married. If you have any doubt about how to address a letter it is always best to check first. See also **Letter Writing** in Basic Rules.

alarms (burglar or car)

If your alarm goes off by accident during the night you should make the effort to apologize to your neighbours, even though it was no fault of yours. By doing so you show them consideration, and indeed, it may be in your best interests to do so because the next time it goes off it could be for 'real' and disgruntled neighbours may pay no attention.

announcements

Local and/or national newspaper announcements can be made for births, engagements, weddings, deaths and other events and celebrations. Check with the newspaper of your choice for the usual layout of their announcements and for an address or telephone number to contact to discuss your announcement.

answering machines

If your call is taken by an answering machine, it is polite to leave a message. Speak clearly, not too quickly and, depending on who you are calling, give your name, the time, date and purpose of your call. Owners of answering machines should respond to these messages as soon as possible. Answering machines are quite often used to 'screen' incoming calls, but it should be borne in mind that some people may find it disconcerting, if not rude, to have their call suddenly answered in the middle of leaving a message.

apologizing

It is not always easy to apologize, but it should be done as graciously and as promptly as possible. If you think someone owes you an apology, let him or her know rather than bearing a grudge. If you think someone expects you to apologize but you do not feel this is fair, discuss the matter with him or her.

applause

Applause is usually welcome but it has its own time and place. There should be no applause between movements in a concert nor should there be spontaneous applause during the course of a play, for example at the entrance of a famous actor or after the delivery of a well-known passage, is not usually acceptable, though it is acceptable to applaud particularly famous opera arias or ballet sequences – often with shouts of 'bravo!' or 'brava!' if the performer is a woman. If you are have any doubt about when to applaud, pay attention to how the rest of the audience respond – applauding alone can be very embarrassing. For most performances which include orchestras (such as concerts, operas, ballets and musicals) the audience will clap when the conductor enters the auditorium and, where applicable, when the soloist or first violinist arrives. If the set for a production is particularly beautiful or innovative the audience may clap as the curtains open.

In most productions the lighting will change or the curtains will come down to mark the end of scenes or acts, and these moments call for applause as does, of course, the end of the performance.

A standing ovation is usually reserved for a particularly outstanding performance. But don't be hesitant, if you think the performance deserved it, stand up – others will probably join you. Particularly well-received productions or sequences may cause the audience to show their appreciation with enthusiastic slow handclapping, or to call 'encore!' in the hopes that the sequence will be repeated.

At the end of a musical performance of any kind never begin clapping until the orchestra has stopped playing. If there are several curtain calls, you should remain until the last one.

arguing in public

You should avoid arguing in public; it humiliates you and those you argue with, and embarrasses people around you. If you have a disagreement in a public place, you should try to deter an argument by saying 'we'll have to talk about this later', or if this is not possible, you should try to find a more private place to carry on your discussion.

artichokes

Artichokes are eaten with the fingers: take each leaf off individually, holding it by the fibrous tip and dip the fleshy, white base in the sauce before scraping the flesh off with your teeth. Discarded leaves should be arranged neatly around the edge of your plate, or put into a separate dish if one has been provided. The tiny leaves towards the centre can be eaten in groups. The fluffy 'choke' should be left and the remaining 'heart' is eaten with a knife and fork. Do not lick your fingers but clean them on your napkin or, if there is one, rinse them first in the finger bowl.

asparagus

Whole asparagus served as a separate dish is eaten with the fingers. Pick each stalk up individually by the tougher, blunt end of the stem and dip the pointed tip into the accompanying sauce. Eat the entire stalk if it is young and tender, but if the end is tough leave it on the side of your plate. Do not lick your fingers but clean them on your napkin or, if there is one, rinse them first in the finger bowl. Asparagus served as an accompaniment to another dish should be eaten with a knife and fork.

At Home cards

These may be used as invitations for many different functions. You can buy blank at home cards or you can have cards printed with your name above the words 'At Home', and your address and/or telephone number under the letters RSVP in the bottom left-hand or right-hand corner. When sending at home cards, add the relevant details, for example: Mrs Edward Morse/ At Home/ on Wednesday 17 September/; and in the bottom corner opposite the RSVP address: suits/ dinner, 7.30 for 8.00.

If you receive an At Home card that gives a telephone number after the letters RSVP, you should reply by telephone. If the address is given, you should reply in writing; you may chose to reply formally, using the formula: Mr Geoffrey Seymour thanks Mrs Edward Morse for her kind invitation, etc.

au pair

An au pair is usually a girl no younger than 17, who has come to the UK to learn English. She should be treated as part of the family and not as an employee, though she will be expected to help out with various chores, such as babysitting or helping with the cleaning. However, her chores must not take up more than five hours a day and she must be allowed one day off a week, and one weekend a month. It is a good idea to specify how your household is run and what her duties will be before she arrives. On top of her board an allowance should also be paid to her.

banns, marriage

In the Church of England, the vicar reads out the banns in church on three successive Sundays. The purpose is to allow anyone who may know of reasons why the marriage should not place to object. If the groom is from another parish he must inform his vicar of the proposed marriage. His vicar will then arrange with bride's vicar that the banns are read in both churches on the same three Sundays. The groom's vicar will then provide a certificate stating that he has read the banns – without this certificate the wedding cannot take place.

Once the banns have been read the marriage may take place at any time within the following three months. However, if the marriage does not take place within this period the banns must be read again. See also **Weddings** in the Special Occasions section and **marriage licences (religious)** in this section.

barbecues

It is polite and considerate to let your neighbours know when you are to have a barbecue, and to try and make sure that it is positioned so that any smoke or fumes do not blow directly into their garden: better still invite them to join in.

beggars

Sadly there are an increasing number of beggars on the streets, and many people feel uncomfortable and intimidated by them. However, there is no reason why they should not be treated with politeness, unless they are particularly aggressive and insistent. If you do not wish to give any money, a simple but firm 'I'm sorry, but I have no change.' is the best way of dealing with them. But if you ignore someone completely they are far more likely to bother you. Some people often carry small change specifically to give away.

belching

We have all been caught out by an unexpected belch and, depending on the occasion, the best thing to do is to laugh it off or apologize and just ignore it. A more formal dinner party is perhaps the most embarrassing situation, but a simple 'excuse me' or 'I beg your pardon' is all that is required while the other guests should continue as though they had not noticed.

bereavement

If you yourself have been bereaved, take things very slowly and don't force yourself to interact with other people until you are ready to. If you need help, let people know – they should be sensitive to your wishes at this very difficult time. When someone you know has been bereaved, check whether you can help with the work that goes with bereavement. Offer your support and visit your bereaved friend, but make sure that you are not a burden to him or her. See also **Funerals and Memorials** in the Special Occasions section.

best man

The chief duties of a best man are to make sure that the groom gets to the church on time; to look after the ring; and to make a speech during the reception. He may also be needed as a general usher and stage manager, making sure that all the right people are in the right place at the right time for the photographs, the speeches, the cutting of the cake and the departure of the bride and groom.

For obvious reasons the best man should be a close friend of the groom. Traditionally, he was a bachelor, though it is now perfectly acceptable for the best man to be married. See also **Weddings** in the Special Occasions section.

birth announcements

See **announcements** in this section.

black tie

'Black tie' means a man's black dinner suit also known as evening dress – a matching black jacket and trousers, often trimmed with satin – worn with a white shirt and black bow tie. You may wear either a black cummerbund or a black waistcoat, but never both together: if you have a double-breasted jacket you do not need to wear either. It has become increasingly popular to wear brightly coloured bow ties, perhaps with a matching cummerbunds or a colourful waistcoats. Both socks and shoes must be black. See also **white tie** in this section and **Correct Clothes** in Basic Rules.

blind people (helping)

In most instances, especially if they have a guide dog, blind people are perfectly capable of coping for themselves. However, they may be grateful for assistance when negotiating stairs, for example at a busy train station, finding a seat on a crowded bus, or trying to cross a road where there is fast moving traffic. The best approach is to ask whether they would like some help, then hold their arm and speak clearly when directing their steps.

blunders

If you make a blunder of some sort – for example by saying something that is offensive or hurtful to someone that you are talking to – you should apologize immediately, but with as little fuss as possible. You should then introduce another topic of conversation, however trivial, to avoid causing offence a second time.

boasting

It is not polite to boast of one's achievements or abilities. If you have done something of which you are proud and want to tell people about it, it is best to introduce the subject by saying 'I'm very lucky because . . . '.

borrowing

Borrowing, especially money, can put considerable strain on friendships. Never ask to borrow something unless you are sure that the person you are asking does not mind, and that you can return the item at the appointed time and in the same state in which it was leant to you; and never borrow anything without asking permission first.

Asking for something to be returned can often be difficult and embarrassing, both for the lender and the borrower. So always be tactful and polite, and avoid turning the issue into an argument.

bosses (deference towards)

However relaxed your working relationship with your boss, you should still show him or her some degree of deference. This shows that you respect the hierarchy of the company and your boss's own achievements. See also **Office Etiquette** in Basic Rules.

bottles (taking to parties)

'Bring-a-bottle' parties have popularized the custom of taking bottles to parties. A bottle is almost invariably welcomed by hosts, especially at larger, informal parties. If, however, you take a bottle to a dinner or lunch party, you should not expect it to be drunk during the course of the meal as your hosts will almost certainly have bought wine to go with the meal. It is also potentially embarrassing, for you or your host, if you have brought a wine far superior to the one being served.

bouquets

See **flowers** in this section.

brandy and liqueurs

These should be offered once the coffee has been served, whether you remain at the table or move to the sitting room. The host should ask his guests whether they would like a liqueur and to tell them what selection he has: common liqueurs would be something like Cointreau, Drambuie or Grand Marnier. See also **port** in this section.

bread rolls

You should use your fingers, not a knife, to break up a roll into small pieces, which you may then butter if you wish.

breakages

If you break something you should admit it and apologize immediately (never hide the evidence in the hope that you will not be discovered). You should also offer to pay for the article to be replaced or repaired.

breakfast

If someone breaks something in your house, try not to make too much of a fuss, however valuable or loved the item was (the 'culprit' will already be feeling sufficiently embarrassed). The main thing with all accidents is too avoid disrupting everyone else. Ideally, you should dismiss the incident and refuse to accept payment for the article if it is offered.

breakfast
When you have house guests to stay the best way to approach breakfast is in a relaxed and informal way. Give your guests an idea of when breakfast will be and keep the meal simple. The easiest thing to do is to make it more of a 'self-service' meal, providing a selection of cereals, spreads, toast, croissants, tea or coffee, whatever. Most people are quite happy to have a simple light breakfast. Bear in mind though that if your guests are not close friends they may be uncomfortable about rummaging around your kitchen, so always be on hand to make extra toast or coffee.

breastfeeding
You should avoid breastfeeding your baby in public. Nursing mothers should respect the fact that people may find breastfeeding offensive or embarrassing, and they should find somewhere private to breastfeed.

bridesmaids
A bride may be attended by any number of bridesmaids, and it is up to the bride to decide what they should wear, but – as the cost of their clothes is often borne by the bridesmaids or their families – she should give them some say in what they wear.

The main function of bridesmaids is to look decorous and, if the bride has a very long train and/or veil, to carry these as the bride advances along the aisle. Flower girls literally carry bouquets, hoops or balls of flowers. Bridesmaids can be of any age, although the very young may be more disruptive than enchanting. Married women may also attend the bride; they are known as matrons of honour.

Amongst the bride's attendants there should be one bridesmaid – usually the oldest, or a close friend or relation of the bride – who will be the chief bridesmaid, and she has several duties to fulfil. She is usually expected to help the bride dress and to keep her calm immediately before leaving the house to go to the church. Before, during and after the service she should keep all the younger attendants under control and make sure that they know what they are meant to be doing. During the service she will take the bride's bouquet and she may help the bride to lift her veil at the relevant moment; if the bride is to give the groom a ring, this may be entrusted to the chief bridesmaid until it is needed in the service. See also **Weddings** in Special Occasions.

business cards

In most Western countries there are no rigid rules of etiquette regarding the use of business cards, other than being useful reminders of people you may have met a trade fair for instance. However, in Japan the exchange of business cards is an essential part of any business meeting. A British businessman should have his card printed in both English and Japanese, and on receiving the card the Japanese will bow.

buskers

Whether or not you give money to buskers is entirely up to you, but if you are particularly impressed by someone and you stop to watch and listen it is only polite to give something for the performance you have enjoyed.

buttonholes

A buttonhole is a tiny bouquet or single bloom – usually a rose or carnation – worn on a man's lapel for formal occasions. At a wedding, the groom should supply buttonholes for himself, his best man and the ushers.

canapés

These are small, savoury snacks served with drinks. Ideally, they should be small enough to be eaten in one mouthful, and not so messy that they dirty guests' hands. Messy or greasy snacks, or those that are dipped into sauces should be served on cocktail sticks.

cancellations

If you have to cancel a wedding, dinner or other function, advise all those that have been invited in writing as soon as possible. If the cancellation occurs at the last moment, guests will have to be contacted by telephone. If a wedding is cancelled or an engagement broken off, you may put an announcement in a newspaper to the effect that the wedding 'will not now be taking place'.

candles

A candlelight dinner is extremely attractive and atmospheric, but don't make it too dark, especially at a more formal dinner party. You must always make sure that there is enough light for people to see what they are eating. It is customary to use white candles at a formal dinner, and remember that, in general, the shorter the candlestick the longer the candle.

carving

Meat may be carved at the table or in the kitchen before serving.

cashpoints (queuing)

When queuing at a cashpoint, especially those situated outside, you should not crowd the person using the machine, give them space and, in a sense, some privacy to conduct their business. For reasons of security as well as politeness, you must never look over their shoulder as they punch in their number or read their balance on the screen.

cheese course
In the UK the cheese course is traditionally served after the dessert; it is equally acceptable to serve it before – or instead of – dessert.

chivalrous gestures
Many men are brought up to show deference to women by standing when they come into the room, holding doors for them and offering them seats. If a man behaves courteously towards a woman this can in no way be interpreted as a threat to her independence, but as a sign of esteem; the gesture should be acknowledged with gratitude.

choking
If you do find yourself choking on a piece of food or drink try to deal with it without too much disruption, use your napkin to cover your mouth and turn away from the table – if necessary quietly get up and excuse yourself. If someone chokes next to you the best thing is to make sure that it isn't serious and to continue with your conversation.

The key to avoiding choking on food is to pay some attention to how much and what you are eating, particularly dry, crumbly food.

chopsticks
Chopsticks should be held in the right hand, in the curve between the thumb and index finger, one is held steady by the middle and third finger and the other placed above it and moved

by the index finger and thumb. However, there is some skill involved in using chopsticks and a certain amount of practice is required before you can use them with ease. If you don't feel confident, it is perfectly acceptable to use a knife and fork.

christening gifts

Godparents and close family members usually give christening presents that have lasting value: a piece of silver or jewellery, perhaps a savings account opened in the child's name. Other guests are not expected to bring presents; if they do, something more immediately useful – such as clothes or a toy – would be appropriate. See also **Christenings** in Special Occasions.

Christmas

Where to spend Christmas is often a problem and a cause for ill feeling. For an engaged couple and especially for newly-weds a certain amount of consideration and thought should be given about whose parents they should visit at Christmas; unless, of course, they have decided to spend Christmas on their own. Often the best policy is either to alternate each year, or, if distance allows, to spend time with both sets of parents over the Christmas period.

cigarettes

See **smoking** in this section.

cinemas

Although going to a cinema is far more informal than the theatre or a concert performance, you should still show consideration for other people in the audience. The most important thing is not to be noisy, in particular don't talk during the film because this is very distracting and annoying for those sitting near you. Try to avoid having to leave your sit once the film has begun, but if you do always thank people for moving out of the way and move down the aisle as quickly as you can. It is best to have your back to the screen when you are getting past people to make sure that you don't step on bags or feet.

cocktail parties

Traditionally a cocktail party is just that, a party at which a selection of cocktails is served. The term is now more loosely applied to evening or pre-lunch drinks parties. See **Parties and Entertaining** in Special Occasions.

coffee

After a meal coffee is served to round off a lunch or dinner, and it is usually served in small coffee cups, although mugs or tea cups may be acceptable on less formal occasions. The coffee may be served at the table or in another room and it may be accompanied by liqueurs and chocolates or other confectionery. It is increasingly common for hosts to offer decaffeinated coffee or tea as an alternative to coffee.

coffee morning

This is a cheap and pleasant way for people to keep in touch. Guests are usually invited by telephone, and the invitation is for 10.30 or 11.00. Coffee is served with a choice of cakes and biscuits. Guests are expected to leave by 12.00 or 12.30.

complaints

If you are moved to complain about something in any situation, you should do so as quietly and politely as possible. A discreet, courteous complaint will be dealt with more graciously than an impetuous one. If you want to complain about something in a public place, such as a restaurant, it is best to leave those you are with and to discuss the matter privately with the staff.

compliments

The best way to accept a compliment is to thank the person who has given it.

When a man takes a woman out it is polite for him to compliment her on her appearance; it is also polite for guests to compliment their hosts on their home and/or the meal they have provided. Compliments should, however, come from the heart.

computer etiquette

Although the use of computers, especially at work, is dictated by office and business practice rather than etiquette, it is important to remember that if you are using someone else's machine you should respect their privacy. A personal computer will usually contain private and confidential material, such as letters, and just as you should not rifle through someone's desk so you should not enter files without permission and certainly not tamper with or delete them.

confetti

Many vicars and hosts no longer like to have confetti thrown on their premises. It is acceptable for wedding invitations to include a note asking guests not to throw confetti, or the vicar may announce at the beginning of the wedding service that he would rather confetti was not thrown in or around the church. Rice or rose petals offer traditional, biodegradable alternatives to confetti.

confirmation

Confirmation is an attestation of commitment to the Christian faith. People may be confirmed in the Christian faith when they feel ready to assume the vows made by their godparents at the time of their christening. Only those who have been christened may be confirmed (those who have never been christened but wish to profess their faith, may have a combined baptism and confirmation service).

confirmation gifts
Godparents, close friends and relations often like to give a confirmation candidate a small gift. These gifts should relate to the religious nature of the ceremony; they may choose, for example, a prayer book or crucifix.

congratulations
If you wish to congratulate someone on some achievement or, for example, on his or her engagement, you should do so as soon as you hear the news. You may choose to telephone him or her or to send a card or brief letter.

conversation
When you meet people for the first time you will inevitably find yourself asking simple questions, such as 'how do you know so-and-so?', 'where do you live?' and 'what do you do?' You may feel self-conscious using these formulae but they are the easiest ways of starting a conversation. Once you or the other person has replied to the opening question you should, however, try to build on this answer to develop a conversation rather than falling back on other 'opening gambit' questions.

It is often said that certain subjects, such as religion or politics, should be avoided, particularly at dinner parties or slightly more formal occasions where all the guests may not know each other well. However, such subjects can usually be certain of stimulating conversation, which is the key to a successful party, but a good host or hostess will make sure that no one becomes too heated, upset or even bored. He or she should always be ready to step in and discreetly steer the course of the conversation on to something less contentious or more interesting.

Gossip it not always a good topic of conversation, especially if it is malicious or if it excludes other guest by being about people or places that they do not know. See also **Introductions** in Basic Rules.

contraception

In today's society it is important to be responsible and open about contraception. It is crucial that you are able and willing to discuss it with your partner. Whatever situation or relationship you are involved in you should always be prepared, it shows that you care not only about yourself but about your partner as well.

corn on the cob

This is usually served without any cutlery, but occasionally with forks which are pushed into each end, otherwise hold it with your fingers and bite the corn off. It is almost impossible to eat corn on the cob without a certain amount of mess, so bear this in mind when planning your menu for a dinner party.

corsage

A corsage is a tiny bouquet or single bloom – such as a rose or orchid – pinned to the breast of a woman's outfit for a smart function. A man may offer his partner at a ball a corsage as a token of his esteem.

coughing

When you cough in public you should always put your hand over your mouth. At a meal you should avert your head from the table and, if you are overcome by coughing, you should leave the table discreetly until you have recovered. During performances of any kind you should keep coughing to a minimum so as not to inconvenience other spectators; if you have a tickle in your throat it is best to clear it with a good cough than to try and suppress it with repeated little coughs.

country code

If you are walking in the country you must adhere to a few, simple rules. You should always keep to the public footpaths and bridle paths, unless you have the farmer's or landowner's permission to walk elsewhere. Always bear in mind that all farmland is private land. Never walk across a field where crops are growing, keep to the sides otherwise you may do considerable damage. Always make sure that you close gates behind you, especially in a field where there are animals. Dogs must be kept under close control; if you are near or walking through a field where there are animals, particularly sheep, keep your dog on its lead.

crab

When eating a whole crab you will be provided with a pair 'nutcrackers' to break open the legs, and a small implement with two hooks at the end to scoop out the flesh. This is also used to get at the flesh in the crab's under section. Crabs are quite messy to eat but do not lick your fingers, clean them on your napkin or, if there is one, rinse them first in the finger bowl. However, it is usual for crab to be served already dressed.

cremations

To have a body cremated you need two doctor's certificates (or a coroner's certificate if the death was referred to the coroner) as well as a signed certificate from the medical representative at the crematorium and a signed application form from the next of kin.

Crematoria are usually small, and cremations are traditionally attended only by immediate family and very close friends. Most crematoria are non-denominational – although many can recommend a Church of England vicar to take the service. The family may invite a clergyman of their choice to officiate, or a cremation need not involve a religious ceremony at all.

The ashes may be buried at the crematorium, in which case a small space has to be bought; they may be interred in a graveyard – perhaps in the grave of a close relation or even a family grave; they may be scattered; or they may be kept in an urn.

Those who attend cremations should be quiet even before and after the ceremony: there may be another cremation taking place immediately before or after the one you are attending and it would be very distressing for the mourners to hear people chatting outside the little chapel. As with funerals people tend to wear dark clothes at cremations and many women choose to wear hats. Flowers are not usually brought to cremations unless the casket is to be buried at the crematorium. Small bouquets from the immediate family are usually laid on the coffin. See also **Funerals and Memorials** in Special Occasions.

criticism

It is impolite to criticize under almost any circumstances. If you have been invited to criticize something by a close friend or in a professional capacity, or if you feel you can't let something pass without criticizing it, you should do so as tactfully as possible and should offer constructive comments to accompany your criticism.

It is important to learn to accept criticism graciously, especially if you have invited it in the first place. If you feel someone's criticism is not justified, you should of course defend your opinion, but make sure that you have a valid defence and are not just trying to salvage your pride.

cutlery

Cutlery should be laid in the order in which it will be needed during a meal, with cutlery for the first course to the outside of the place setting and for the last course on the inside. If there is a knife to the far right-hand side of the place setting this is for buttering bread rolls on your side plate.

Forks: these are laid to the left-hand side of the place setting, with the tines facing upwards. Dessert forks may be laid immediately above the place setting, with the tines to the right and the handle to the left. Forks are almost always used in conjunction with a knife. The fork should be held with the handle nestling in the left hand, the first finger pointing along to the root of the tines, and the thumb and second finger clamping it in place. The tines should point downwards onto the plate and should prong the food so that it does not fall off on its way to the mouth. The fork should not be used as a 'shovel' – although in informal situations this is acceptable for rice and peas – and should never be turned over in the right hand and used to cut food.

Knives: these should be laid to the right-hand side of the place setting with the blade facing inwards. Small butter knives may be laid on the side plate. A knife should be held so that its handle nestles in the right hand with the first finger pointing along the top of the handle towards the blade; the thumb and second finger clamp the handle in place. The knife should only be used for cutting food and for pushing it onto the downturned prongs of the fork. It should not be used for shovelling food, and should never be brought to the mouth.

Spoons: these are laid on the right-hand side of the place setting with the bowl facing upwards. The dessert spoon may be laid above the place setting in which case it is laid above the fork, with the bowl to the left hand side. Always make sure you have enough serving spoons for the number of dishes you are serving. If you are putting serving dishes on the table for guests to help

dancing

themselves, lay the spoon to one side of the serving dish. See also **Table Manners** in Basic Rules and **Dinner Parties** in Special Occasions.

dancing
It is perfectly acceptable nowadays to dance alone at clubs or discos. A request to dance should always be polite, as should a refusal. Never start dancing with someone without asking first, and do not bother anyone on the dance floor after a refusal has been made. When dancing to slower records maintain a distance between you and your partner, and never assume that your partner wants to continue dancing – always ask first.

deaf people (talking to)
If you are talking to someone who is profoundly deaf it may not help just raising your voice, instead make sure that you are facing them when you speak and speak slowly, enunciating your words clearly. With a little effort and thought on your part most deaf people are more than capable of following a conversation.

death announcements
See **announcements** in this section.

death (registering)
When a person dies a doctor should be contacted immediately. He or she will supply the death certificate which has to be taken to the register office within two weeks of the death, in order to register the death. See also **Funerals and Memorials** in Special Occasions.

dentists
It is only polite to show some consideration for your dentist by not eating just before you go (avoid particularly pungent foods,

like garlic, perhaps even a day or so before an appointment) and to brush your teeth. It is embarrassing for you and unpleasant for the dentist, if your mouth reeks of your last meal. It will also hamper the investigation or treatment if there are bits of food still in your mouth.

diets (special needs)
If you are a vegetarian, have food allergies or have any other special dietary needs and are invited out for a meal you should let your hosts know when you accept their invitation. If you are travelling on a journey during which a meal will be provided, contact the travel company in advance to warn them of your special dietary needs.

dogs (in public places)
You must always keep your dog on a lead when you are walking in a town, and you must always clean up any mess that it makes, especially on pavements and in parks where children may be playing. In most parks you are allowed to let your dog off the lead, but make sure that it doesn't bother or annoy anyone. See also **pets** in this section.

dropping in
If you drop in on someone you should not do so before 10 in the morning or after 6 in the evening. Always ask whether it is a good time. If your friend says it is not – or hesitates before replying – you should leave straight away, perhaps making a date for a future visit. In any event, you should only stay about 30 minutes, and not more than an hour, unless your host presses you to stay on. It is best not to drop in unannounced on someone who you do not know very well, with such a person you should always ring to check whether it would be convenient; dropping in is very much something you do with close friends.

drunks (dealing with)

This can often be a tricky situation to deal with, depending on the state of the inebriated person and the occasion. If someone is disrupting your party, the best thing to do is to politely but firmly manoeuvre him or her out of the room, with assistance if required, and let them either sleep it off upstairs or get them a taxi home. Try to avoid an embarrassing scene and don't let it ruin your whole party.

elbows on table

Elbows should not be put on the table, although the lower arm may be rested lightly on the table. There are two good reasons for this: first, you may knock things over or even unbalance the table; second, it stops conversation between your neighbours. See also **Table Manners** in Basic Rules.

elderly people

In whatever situation, elderly people deserve consideration, patience and respect. Always be ready to offer assistance, whether crossing a road or helping to carry a bag up some stairs. On buses or trains you should always offer your seat.

embarrassment

If you are involved in any kind of embarrassing scene – such as an argument or a child's tantrum – you should apologize to those around you immediately, but briefly. Don't add to the fuss by apologizing at length.

Scenes that may humiliate you or embarrass those around you should be avoided at all costs. If, for example, you are tempted to argue with someone in a public place you should either agree to differ until you have an opportunity to discuss the matter privately, or move somewhere where your disagreement will not embarrass anyone else.

It is natural to feel embarrassment in certain circumstances; most people will understand this so there should be little need to conceal these feelings. The best way to overcome embarrassment is to forget the incident or remark that caused it and move on to something else.

engagements

When a couple become engaged it is usual to congratulate the man and to wish the woman every happiness. You can either ring or send a card or letter with your best wishes. There is no need to have an engagement party, but some couples like to announce their engagement at a large party where all their friends can meet.

If an engagement is broken off, the girl should return her engagement ring (especially if she broke off the engagement), and any engagement presents that the couple may have received. If wedding invitations have already been issued, a note should be sent to all the guests saying that the wedding will no longer be taking place; and any wedding presents that have already been received should be returned with a note of thanks and regret. See **Engagements** in Special Occasions.

entertaining

Entertaining should be a pleasant way of making and keeping friends, and it should not be an ordeal for the hosts. You should only really invite people whom you would like to get to know as friends, and you should plan any form of entertainment carefully so that you will have time on the day to enjoy it as much as your guests.

Business entertaining, may not be as pleasurable as entertaining one's own friends, but it should still not be an ordeal. The object of the exercise is to build a more familiar and relaxed relationship with colleagues, clients and other business associates. Whether you choose to entertain business associates at home or elsewhere, you should plan the event carefully so that you have enough time to become involved in the conversation. See also **Introductions** in Basic Rules; **Dinner Parties**, **House Guests**, **Parties and Entertaining**, **Restaurant Meals** and **Theatre Trips and Other Outings** in Special Occasions.

esquire

The suffix esquire – usually abbreviated to Esq. – is traditionally used when addressing an envelope to a man. It cannot be used in conjunction with any title or rank, but is often used instead of the title 'Mr', for example, James Gillespie, Esq.

evening dress

When an invitation stipulates that guests should wear evening dress, this means that the men should be in 'black tie' (functions that require men to wear 'white tie' – known as full evening dress – will make this clear on the invitation). Ladies should wear long or calf-length dresses or skirts, although above the knee hemlines are also acceptable. See **black tie** and **white tie** in this section; see also **Correct Clothes** in Basic Rules.

ex partners

However acrimonious a break up you may have had with a part-ner, you should be civil when you meet him or her. If you feel you cannot be polite to your ex, you should make every effort not to meet him or her, and should steer clear of him or her if you are both invited to the same function.

It is best to avoid talking about ex's with present partners. Such talk can engender jealousy and it can even paint an unat-tractive picture of you yourself.

faxes

A fax is somewhere between an informal letter and a telephone call, and should be used accordingly. The basic form of a fax is a written communication and so some of the rules of letter writing apply, but it is instantly communicated and so you should follow the guidelines of telephone etiquette: for example, identify yourself and the purpose of the fax clearly, and don't tie up someone's machine with an enormous fax without prior warning.

finger bowls

Small bowls of water can be a great help for cleaning fingers after eating asparagus or artichokes, for example. Finger bowls are usually laid individually, just above the place setting. The water may be warm or cold and may be made slightly fragrant with a slice of lemon or some rose petals. The tips of the fingers should be dipped in the water and rubbed gently, and then dried on a napkin.

first names

In most circumstances you will be given people's first names and their surnames when you are introduced to them. If you feel that the person is your equal, it is most natural to use his or her first name. If, however, you feel you owe the person respect – because of his or her age, rank or position – you should use his or her surname until invited to use his or her first name. See also **Introductions** in Basic Rules.

flies (unzipped)

If you notice – or someone points out – that your flies are undone, you should turn away from those with you in order to adjust them. Do not draw attention to the fact by apologizing; and resume the conversation as quickly as possible. If you notice that a friend's flies are undone, you should tell him or her. If you are introduced to a stranger whose flies are undone, you must consider your actions carefully: you may embarrass yourself and the other person more by pointing the fact out than by discreetly ignoring it.

flirting

Many people feel that flirting is harmless, but think before you overindulge. Flirting, however casual, with other people may hurt your partner. Excessive flirting can also become tiresome for other people and it may lead to an embarrassing misunderstanding.

flowers

As a gift: a bouquet of flowers makes a very good gift for a hostess of a dinner, lunch or house party. You may either bring them with you or send them with a letter of thanks afterwards. Flowers can also be given to the sick and the bereaved as a sign of concern and sympathy; they are also one of the most popular gifts given by men to women.

At weddings: the bride's bouquet is traditionally given to her by the groom, although many girls like to chose the flowers themselves. The groom should pay for his bride's bouquets. The posies carried by bridesmaids and flower girls are traditionally paid for by the bride's parents.

At funerals: some families prefer to have only family flowers at funerals, in which case they will probably make this point in a newspaper announcement. If you would like to send a bouquet of flowers for a funeral, it is usual to send them to the undertaker who will lay them by the graveside. You may, of course, take them yourself. If you put a message with the bouquet it should be addressed to the deceased.

food

As a gift: food is often given as a gift, usually chocolate. Chocolates and other confectionery can be taken as thank-you presents
for hostesses of house parties or dinner parties. Food, usually
fresh fruit, is commonly brought as a gift for the sick. Delicacies
and home-made produce may also be given when visiting
friends.

When entertaining: there are several criteria to determine the
choice of food for parties. The first is that the food should come
within your budget. Secondly, you should consider whether the
food will sate your guests without leaving them feeling too full.
Next, you should try to use a variety of different flavours and
textures throughout the meal. Finally, you should make sure
that a good proportion of the food can be prepared in advance so
that you are free to entertain your guests.

Serving: a host may ask guests to help themselves to each
course from a sideboard but it is more traditional to serve them.
You may give guests empty plates and then come round the table
with each dish, serving guests from the left-hand side. It may be
more practical to pass serving dishes around, or to put some or
all of them on the table for guests to help themselves.

Seconds: it is not obligatory to accept the offer of a second
helping, but it may be more polite to do so, particularly if your
host or hostess has gone to a great deal of trouble to cook the
meal you are eating. Equally, it is not essential that you should
cook enough food so as to make sure that there will be enough to
offer seconds.

Spilling, leaving and refusing: if you spill a small amount of
food, you should simply ignore it. If you spill enough to make a
mess, you should apologize and help clear it up, offering to pay
any cleaning bills if this is appropriate. Whatever the circumstances, you should not cause a commotion, and the meal should
be resumed as soon as possible.

Ideally, you should not have to leave any food on your plate. If you have been served too much, or cannot eat something you have been served, put it at the edge of the plate, don't leave it in the middle.

If you don't like a dish that you are offered it is best to take only a small amount and to eat it politely. If you are allergic to something, you should refuse it as discreetly as possible or take a small amount and then leave it on the side of your plate.

Spitting out food: if you must spit out a small amount of food – because it is unpalatable or you cannot chew it – bring your spoon or fork up to your mouth, pop the food onto it and then leave it on the side of your plate.

On how to eat difficult foods, such as artichokes, asparagus, mussels and oysters, see individual entries in this section and see also **Table Manners** in Basic Rules.

forks
See **cutlery** in this section.

formal occasions
Invitations to formal occasions will always indicate when you should arrive and some will stipulate when you should leave. If there is to be a royal guest, the invitation may indicate when he or she will arrive, and you should make a point of arriving before this time. You should not leave a formal occasion before the guest of honour has left, neither should you linger on long after he or she has gone. It is, however, acceptable to leave a royal garden party before the Queen leaves. The invitation will also state what clothes should be worn, for example, 'black tie' or 'white tie'. See **Formal and Royal Occasions** in Special Occasions.

fruit

Fruit may be served in the place of a dessert course or as a separate course, after the cheese course.

Eating: because pears are potentially quite juicy and so messy to eat, it is best, especially at a formal meal, to quarter and then peel the pear with the fruit knife rather than just biting into it whole. Apples should also be eaten this way, but only at the most formal of occasions.

Eating an orange is usually quite messy and the best way to tackle one is to peel it with a knife, then divide it into segments and eat the segments with your fingers. However, at exceptionally formal dinners it is traditional to eat an unpeeled orange with a knife and fork.

The best way of dealing with pips is to put your hand to your mouth and then, without spitting, let the pips fall into your hand. The pips should then be discarded onto the edge of your fruit plate. See also **food** in this section.

funerals

Clothes: it is a sign of respect to wear sober colours and only discreet jewellery at funerals and cremations. Some men wear a 'black tie' or a black armband, and women may like to wear a hat, possibly with a veil.

Refreshments: afterwards after a funeral the chief mourner may invite other mourners for some form of refreshment. This may be a formal meal for a set number of people in a restaurant, or a casual drink for anyone and everyone attending the service. The atmosphere depends on the setting and the mood of the chief mourner; it should not be riotous, but need not be cheerless. See **Funerals and Memorials** in Special Occasions.

fur coats

For those people who wear fur it should be borne in mind that an increasing number of people consider such clothing as quite unacceptable, and (as with non-smokers) are less and less inhibited in saying so.

However, even if you do find the wearing of fur abhorrent you should try to balance your principles with politeness; if you are not able to bite your tongue at least confine your comments to a polite, calm expression of your opinion.

garlic

Bear in mind that garlic is a food with a lingering pungency, which many people find quite unpleasant. If after eating garlic you know that you may be in close proximity to other people, such as a meeting or at a party, try to diminish the effect with mints, etc.

gatecrashers

If you notice that strangers have gatecrashed your party you should approach them and ask them quietly to leave so as not to disrupt the atmosphere. If they do not respond to this polite request you should let them know that you will contact the police if they persist in staying; you should not hesitate to contact the police if they are not intimidated by this threat.

It is unacceptable to attend a function to which you have not been invited. If you desperately want to attend, your only hope is to ask someone who has been invited to 'put in a good word for you' with the hosts, in the hopes that they will then invite you.

gifts

Whether a gift is a sign of love or a token of gratitude try to make sure that it is appropriate: if you go to stay with someone who has just moved house, give him or her something useful or attractive for the household; if you visit a friend who has just given birth, give her something for the baby. When you are invited out for a meal, you are not expected to take a present, but many guests like to take chocolates or flowers.

Birthday presents are often difficult; try to make presents relevant to the person's interests and hobbies. Wedding presents are sometimes the easiest because so many couples have wedding lists (see **Weddings** in the Special Occasions section). Unless you know the couple especially well and are sure they will like something you have chosen for them, it is safest to choose a present from their list: this will avoid embarrassing doubling up of presents, and will ensure they get the things they need for their new life. Whoever you are buying a present for, remember that it is always best to get something small and appropriate. See also, **Christenings** and **Christmas Cards and Presents** in Special Occasions.

glasses

Laying glasses: they should be placed on the right-hand side of the place setting, just above the knives. Ideally there should be one glass for each different wine to be served, as well as a water glass. Brandy and liqueur glasses can be brought to the table at the appropriate time.

If your glass tends to become very smudged with fingerprints and/or lip marks during the course of a meal, you should hold the glass as close to its base as possible and should dab your mouth on your napkin before drinking.

gloves

If you are wearing gloves and you are introduced to someone who is not, you should remove your gloves to shake hands, although some women's gloves are so tight-fitting that this is impractical. Women's evening gloves should be removed only for eating.

Glyndebourne

An opera festival held in the summer, from May to August.
Audiences at Glyndebourne are expected to wear evening dress
– the men 'black tie' and women full-length dresses. Although if
they are having a picnic outside they should make sure that they
have suitably warm and waterproof coats.

godparents

Choosing and asking: the godparents of your child should themselves have been baptized, and they should be people who will
show an interest in the child's growth and upbringing. Preferably, they should be close and trustworthy friends and should
see the child regularly.

Godparents' duties: during the service godparents are asked to
affirm their faith and confirm their commitment to see their godchild brought up in that faith; at some time during the ceremony, they should each hold the baby.

Godparents are primarily intended to ensure that their godchild is brought up in the Christian faith. Less importance is
now attached to the religious aspect of their responsibilities, but
they should take an interest in the child's happiness and
upbringing. Ideally, they should see the child often, and should
make a point of remembering birthdays and Christmas.

Godparents' gifts: at the time of the christening, godparents
usually give presents that have lasting value: a piece of silver or
jewellery, perhaps a savings account opened in the child's name.
For ensuing birthdays and Christmases they may give gifts that
the child can appreciate more immediately, such as toys or clothes. See also **Christenings** in Special Occasions.

golf

The most important rule in golf is to make sure that your shots
do not endanger anyone: always check before you address the
ball, and if in doubt call 'fore!' as a warning.

If you are holding up the players behind you on the course, let them pass however exciting your game is, and always leave the greens promptly to let other players onto them. Players are usually expected to make good any damage they do to the course and the greens as they go along.

gossip
However apparently harmless, gossip can be hurtful and it can backfire on its perpetrator. See **conversation** in this section.

grace
It is, of course, up to you whether to say grace at the beginning of a meal, but if a clergyman is present (especially if he has just officiated at, for example, a christening service) it is polite to invite him to say grace.

guests
Guest rooms: a room should be warm but well aired; the bed(s) should be made; towels and drinking water should be provided; and cupboard space with hangers made available. Flowers, biscuits, magazines and even a radio may also be put in the room.

Mixing guests: when planning any kind of entertainment you should ensure that the guests you have chosen will mix well together, especially if you are planning only a small gathering; for example, don't invite one very quiet person amongst a crowd of rowdy friends.

Sleeping arrangements: single guests should be given a room of their own and married couples must be put in a room together. Most hosts allow engaged couples to share a room and many will put unmarried couples together too, but it is your house and you may do as you see fit. If you are not sure of the relationship between a man and a woman, ask the woman whether she would like to share a room with the man; or put them in rooms that are

185

close together. If you decide to put a couple together without asking them, put them in twin beds rather than a double bed. If you have to have guests sharing rooms, always put people of the same sex together and make younger guests share rather than older ones.

Uninvited guests: if someone drops in on you at an awkward moment, it is quite acceptable to let them know that you cannot see them. If someone brings an uninvited friend with them to a party, it is best to grit your teeth and accept this uninvited guest rather than causing a scene (see **gatecrashers** in this section). See also **House Guests** in Special Occasions.

handkerchiefs

It is advisable to carry a handkerchief at all times. Handkerchiefs can be kept in a pocket or bag, or just inside the cuff. Traditionally, a handkerchief should not be kept in the breast pocket of a suit.

handshaking

The handshake is a fairly formal greeting and should be treated with respect. You should shake hands firmly but not vigorously and you should not ignore an outstretched hand that has been proffered for a handshake.

hats

Men may wear hats on any occasion, but a man should remove his hat when he goes indoors (except when entering a synagogue). Women may wear hats on any occasion, and they need not remove them when they go indoors.

Henley Royal Regatta

The regatta is held every year during the beginning of July. The Stewards' Enclosure at Henley Royal Regatta stipulates that men should wear a jacket or blazer (which they must not remove) and a tie or cravat. Women are not permitted to enter the enclosure if they are wearing trousers, denim, culottes or above-knee-length skirts. However, you can only get into the Stewards' Enclosure if you are invited, though you can also watch from the Regatta Enclosure or from the public section of the river bank.

hen parties
There is no need for an engaged girl to have a hen party before she is married. If she chooses to have one – usually a meal out with a number of friends – it is customary for the matron of honour to organize the event.

hiccups
Persistent hiccups can be very embarrassing and difficult to deal with discreetly at a formal dinner party. If you feel that they are not going to pass off quickly, excuse yourself from the table and try to get rid of them using whatever method works for you. The occasional, isolated hiccup should be dealt with as with belching, possibly with an apology but in general it is best just to ignore it. See **belching** in this section.

horses
When passing horses in a car you must always slow down, give them space and avoid doing anything that might upset or frighten them. On the whole, wherever you are or however much room there is, you should always give precedence to the horse.

If you are riding on the road it is polite to thank a driver with a simple wave when they have slowed down for you.

hospital visits

See **visits** in this section or **Visting the Sick** in Special Occasions.

hosts

The most important duty of a host is to ensure that his or her guests have everything they need. Guests should be introduced to each other if they have not met, and generally made to feel at home. See **Dinner Parties, House Guests** and **Parties and Entertaining** in Special Occasions.

hotels

Booking: most hotel rooms should be booked in advance to avoid disappointment. At the time of booking you may be asked for a deposit.

Staying in: hotel guests should observe the regulations of the establishment and should respect the needs of other guests; they should be quiet in the corridors, especially late at night and early in the morning. Hotel staff should be treated as professionals not as servants and any complaints should be dealt with discreetly.

Hotel staff: doormen, porters and room service staff may be given a small tip when they provide a service. Chambermaids may be left a tip in the room at the end of a stay.

housewarming parties

If you are invited to a housewarming party it is polite to take a gift that will be of some use to your friends in their new home.

indiscretions

If you make indiscreet remarks about yourself you may well regret it later. You should never be indiscreet about your friends; this amounts to betraying their confidence.

interviews
See **Interview Etiquette** in Special Occasions.

introductions
Introducing oneself: if you are in a situation that requires you to introduce yourself to people, wait for a suitable pause in their conversation and step forward, preferably offering your hand to shake to the person who last spoke. Give your name and, if appropriate, surname and/or title, and tell them something about yourself that will help them to start up a conversation with you, or pick up on a point that was made in their conversation.

Introducing children: children should be introduced to adults in much the same way as another adult would be. It is up to you and your friends to decide whether your children address your friends by their first names or surnames.

Names to use: in formal and business situations you should always introduce people using their surnames as well as their first names. Even in a more relaxed environment it is best to give first names and surnames.

Remembering names: when you are introduced to someone, repeat his or her name as you shake hands or say hello. It is also helpful to associate a person's name with something distinctive about him or her. See also **Introductions** in Basic Rules.

invitations
Details on invitations: state who has sent it and to whom it is addressed. It should give a time, date and place and some indication of what sort of function it entails, for example, drinks, dinner or a dance. It should also state what guests are expected to wear, and have a telephone number or address for replies.

When to send: wedding invitations are usually sent out about six weeks in advance. Invitations for balls and formal occasions should be sent out between a month and six weeks in advance.

Invitations for dances should go out about three weeks in advance. Written invitations for dinner parties and drinks parties should be sent two or three weeks in advance. Telephone invitations can be given a little nearer the time.

For details on accepting and refusing, see **Letter Writing** in Basic Rules.

jewellery

In general, the wearing of jewellery and the type worn depends on whether it is appropriate for the occasion. For example, very brash, over-the-top jewellery would probably not be appropriate for most job interviews and it would certainly be unacceptable at a funeral. There is also an element of practicality, for instance, dangling jewellery that makes some kind of noise would not be suitable at a concert performance.

jokes

Before you tell a joke you should consider the company you are in. Many people are offended by sexist and racist jokes or jokes that include foul language.

kilts

See **Scottish formal dress** in ths section.

kissing

Obviously there is no harm in pecking someone on the cheek in public, but you should not indulge in protracted intimate or passionate kissing in front of other people, especially if this means leaving one person as 'gooseberry'.

Many people kiss once or twice on the cheek as a greeting and a farewell. If someone steps forward to kiss you in this way, it is impolite not to reciprocate.

knives
See **cutlery** in this section.

lateness
See **punctuality** in this section.

laughter
It is polite to laugh at a joke, even if you don't find it especially funny (unless, of course, you find it offensive); but you should never laugh at someone else's expense and should not laugh so loudly that, for example, you disturb other diners in a restaurant.

lavatories
Lavatories should be left in the state in which you found them. Men should always put the lavatory seat back down after use. Where there is a downstairs 'cloakroom' as well as an upstairs lavatory in a house, men are usually expected to use the cloakroom, leaving the upstairs one free for ladies.

leaving the table
You should not leave the table during the course of a meal. If, however, you choke or feel unwell you should leave the table quietly and return as soon as possible. During very long meals, it is considered acceptable to slip away to the lavatory between courses.

letters
Letters of condolence: these are difficult to write but they provide great comfort. Keep the letter short if you find it difficult and, if possible, include some anecdote that illustrates your fond memories of the deceased. Tell your correspondent that they need not thank you for your letter, therefore relieving them of a

duty but not stopping them if they would like to reply. If you receive letters of condolence, you should reply to them. If you feel unable to, try to find someone who can send a note on your behalf or have some little cards of thanks printed.

Replying to letters: you should always reply to letters promptly, certainly within a week of receiving them. When replying to a business letter, always quote any reference numbers on the letter you have received.

Thank-you letters: these should be written promptly; they need not be long but they should be sincere and enthusiastic. The letter need not deal only with the thing you are thanking for, but it is polite to reiterate your thanks at the end of the letter. If you are sent money you should always send a letter of thanks to act as a receipt. See **Letter Writing** in Basic Rules.

libraries
It is polite to be quiet in libraries so that other people can concentrate on what they are reading.

lifts
When standing in a crowded lift it is polite to respect other peoples' 'space' by not staring at them. Always look down or straight in front of you. If you are by the control buttons you should ask people what floor they want as they enter the lift, and always be ready to hold open the doors. As in most situations, people with prams or elderly people should be given precedence when entering or leaving. Never force your way onto a lift that is already crowded, be patient and wait for the next one.

lingering at parties
If you stay on after many of the guests have left a party, make sure that you are not keeping your hosts up against their will. Get up and say 'I must be going'; they will quickly protest if they

would like you to stay. If you are a host and feel that some guests will never leave, you may let the odd yawn slip out and admit that you are getting tired.

lobster

The flesh of a lobster should be scooped from the shell with a knife and fork, and then cut up and eaten as with any other food. A special pick should be provided to extract the flesh from the claws.

lounge suits

Lounge suits are worn by men for many different occasions: work, job interviews, parties, weddings, christenings and funerals. For more formal occasions, darker coloured suits (but not brown) are more appropriate, and suit jackets should not be removed. If wearing a double-breasted suit you should undo the bottom button when seating down, and re-button it when standing up. Only the middle button on a single-breasted suit should be fastened. Ideally, the jacket should fit to allow half an inch of shirt collar and cuff to show. If you are wearing a waistcoat the bottom button is left unfastened. See also **Correct Clothes** in Basic Rules.

loyal and patriotic toasts

At formal dinners the loyal toast – to the monarch – must always be the first to be proposed. It is proposed by the host or chairman, she or he rises to their feet, raises a glass and says, 'Ladies and gentleman, the Queen'. All the guests then stand up, raise their glasses and respond, 'The Queen'. There may then follow another loyal toast to the royal family, however, this is increasingly less common. It is the Queen who decides the exact form of such a toast, and it is changed from time to time.

At dinners held by the armed forces it is usual for some form of patriotic toast to be made, either to the forces as a whole or to a specific element such as a regiment. For example, the toast may be (usually proposed by the host) 'Ladies and gentlemen, Her Majesty's forces', and the guests stand and respond, 'Her Majesty's forces'.

It is important to remember that at formal occasions you should not smoke until the loyal toast has been made. See also **toasts** in this section.

luggage
On any form of public transport you should never take up seats with your luggage, always be ready to move your bags from a seat if someone wants to sit down. You should also ensure that your luggage is not in anyone's way, particularly in gangways or corridors. Always remember if you are carrying a back-pack or shoulder bag that on a crowded train, platform, bus or queue you can easily knock into someone.

lying
You should avoid lying in all circumstances but especially in a business environment. Very occasionally, you may decide that a little white lie could save someone from embarrassment or hurt.

make-up (applying in public)
It is not considered polite to apply or fix your make-up in public, particularly at the table in a restaurant. You should always excuse yourself and go to the lavatory to 'powder your nose'.

manners (at the table)
See **Table Manners** in the Basic Rules section.

marriage licences (civil)
Superintendent registrar's certificate: in England and Wales a couple may marry in any register office, but one of them must

have been resident in the particular office's district for a minimum of seven days. The superintendent registrar will require documented proof that the couple are of legal age, and if either had been previously married proof of divorce or a death certificate. The documents must be the actual ones, photocopies are not acceptable. If these requirements are met the registrar will then display a notice of marriage for 21 days (there is a fee for this notice). If the bride and groom live in different districts notice must be given to the registrar in both districts. After the 21 days, and if no objection to the marriage has been made, a certificate is issued to either of the couple in person. The marriage can then take place, in a building registered for wedding ceremonies, at any time within three months from the date that notice of the wedding was entered by the registrar.

This certificate is also required for any wedding that is not performed by the Church of England.

Superintendent registrar's licence: such a licence may be sought when a couple, for whatever reason, needs to marry quickly and wishes to avoid the 21 days notice of the wedding.

Either one of the couple must have been a resident in the register office's district for at least 15 days. The marriage must take place in the district that the licence is granted, in a building registered for weddings, and there must be one day between the issue of the licence and the wedding. The couple may then marry within three months from the date of application.

Church of Scotland: a couple may be married in any church of their choosing. The Church of Scotland do not require the reading of banns, but the couple must submit a notice of marriage to the civil registrar at least 15 days before the date, and a Schedule of Marriage will then be issued if the registrar is satisfied. The notice must be signed in front of two witnesses, who must be householders, and who also sign. The notice is then put on view at the registrar's office, of the district in which the couple live, for seven days to allow for anyone to come forward with an objection to the marriage. Once a Schedule is issued it is valid for three months.

The Schedule must be signed after the ceremony by the couple, the minister and two witnesses (over 14), and returned within three days to the registrar.

marriage licences (religious)

In England and Wales there are two types of marriage licence, a common and a special licence:

Common licence: a common licence may be sought when a couple cannot wait the required 21 days it takes to read the banns. The couple apply for the licence through their minister, with the approval of the local diocesan council. One of the couple must be resident in the parish for at least 15 days before the wedding.

A common licence is required when one or both of the couple is not a British citizen or are not resident in England and Wales.

Once the licence is issued the wedding may take place with only one day's notice, and it is valid for three months.

Special licence: a special licence is issued for exceptional circumstances, such as the bride or groom being too ill marry in a church. This licence allows for a marriage to be held at any time and in any place, such as a private chapel, a hospital or any place not authorized for marriage ceremonies. It can only be issued with the approval of the Archbishop of Canterbury.

Scotland: there is no residential qualification for marriages in Scotland. If the bride or groom is a resident of Wales or England a superintendent registrar's certificate is acceptable, and must be applied for in the usual way (see above). The couple must sign a notice of marriage in front of two householders, who must also sign the document. If the registrar is satisfied with the notice, it is then put on view for seven days. After this period, and if no objections have been made, a certificate of publication is issued and the couple may marry at any time within the next three months.

For details about Roman Catholic, Jewish and Nonconformist weddings see **Weddings** in Special Occasions. See also **banns, marriage** in this section.

memorial services

A memorial service may be called a service of remembrance or, in the Roman Catholic faith, a Requiem Mass. Such services are usually held a few days or weeks after the funeral or cremation and they are generally held as a celebration of the life and achievements of a person of some import – although, not necessarily on an international scale.

If you arrange to have a newspaper announcement just after a death you may mention in the announcement that a memorial service will be held, giving the time, date and place. You may like to invite people individually either by telephoning, writing or even sending printed invitations.

Memorial services are usually held in the local church of the deceased or a church that he or she attended regularly. The family should discuss the order of the service and the choice of music, hymns, prayers and readings with the clergyman; they may choose to have service sheets printed. If they would like to invite another vicar to participate in or take the service they should make sure that this is acceptable to the incumbent vicar.

If you are invited to – or choose to – attend a memorial service, you should be smartly and soberly dressed, but not gloomily so; memorial services are often uplifting occasions, intended as celebrations.

money

It is quite acceptable to talk about the economy in general terms, but it is considered indiscreet to discuss your own or someone else's finances in social conversation.

morning dress
Morning dress is a black or grey tail coat worn with matching trousers, a waistcoat, stiff-collared shirt and top hat. A grey cravat can be substituted for a tie. See also **Correct Clothes** in Basic Rules.

museums
Some museums do not charge an entry fee, but they may invite you to make a donation and it is polite to donate even a small sum. When visiting a museum you should always consider the other visitors by keeping quiet and not pushing past other people to look at exhibits.

mussels
When mussels are served in their shells, you may be given a special pick with which to pluck out the flesh, but if not you can pull out the flesh using another shell as pincers.

name-dropping
The only purpose of name-dropping is to impress people, and as such it is a form of boasting and usually fanciful boasting at that. Consequently, it is not considered good social behaviour and anyone who does it is quickly identified as a bore.

napkins
Laying: napkins can be laid on the side plate or in the middle of the place setting; they may be folded simply or ornately.

Using: napkins should be unfolded and laid on your lap soon after you sit down. They should be used to dab the mouth and chin for stray morsels. When the meal is over leave your napkin on the table and don't worry about re-folding it.

noise (neighbours)

Noisy neighbours can be one of the great miseries of modern city life, whether it is someone who regularly has all-night parties, plays their music very loud or owns a dog that barks throughout the day. Initially, the best approach is to politely explain your complaint, it will not help angrily to go round and demand that they be quiet. However, if this course of action fails, you should contact your local Environmental Noise Officer. For an extremely rowdy party you can call the police, but this will not help your relationship with your neighbours.

Conversely, if you plan to have a party which is likely to go on very late it is polite to let your neighbours know. You should also state at what time the party will end, and make sure that you keep to that time limit. If someone does complain you should be sympathetic and apologize, however unreasonable you may think they are.

observing religious beliefs

However peculiar someone else's religious beliefs may seem, we should always respect them. It may seem strange to us that Muslims pray at specific times of day and that Jews do not eat pork, or even that committed Christians are offended by blasphemy, but we should never laugh at another person's faith, it does not do us any harm or cause us inconvenience. If you are really intrigued by another person's religion, he or she shouldn't mind you asking about it, but it is unfair to delve too deeply or to take issue with their doctrines.

When you are travelling, you should respect the religious beliefs of your host nations: some peoples do not accept nudity on beaches, others do not even tolerate bare arms in public.

opening doors

When visiting places of worship you should observe the regulations there, for example, removing shoes before entering a mosque.

opening doors

opening doors

Traditionally, of course, it was expected that a man should open a door for a woman, but today it is really a matter of common courtesy for a man or woman to hold open a door for someone. For example, once you have passed through a swing door in a shop you should always hold it open for the person behind you, especially in a supermarket where that person may be weighed down with bags.

opera

With the exception of galas and first nights, there are no dress stipulations for opera performances. What you choose to wear depends on who you are with and, possibly, how much you spent on your tickets.

oysters

When you eat fresh oysters from the shell, you will be provided with a small fork to lever the flesh out. Use the fork in your right hand and hold the shell down with your left. Once you have prised the flesh free, you may, if you prefer, tip the shell up and empty the flesh straight into your mouth.

pageboys

It is up to the bride to choose, in consultation with the groom, who will be pageboys and to decide what they should wear, but – as the cost of their clothes is usually borne by themselves or their families – she should give them some say in what they wear. It is usual for at least one member of the bridal party to come from the groom's family.

The main function of pageboys is to look decorous and, if the bride has a very long train and/or veil, to carry these as the bride advances along the aisle.

The bride should ask those she would like to be her attendants (and, if they are young, their parents) well in advance and, to avoid embarrassment later, should make it clear who will be paying for their outfits. She should also help the groom to buy a little gift of thanks for each of her attendants; these will be given to them during the reception, possibly during the bridegroom's speech. See **Weddings** in Special Occasions.

parties

Arriving: you should always try to arrive within 20 minutes of the arrival time stated on an invitation, and certainly within 45 minutes. Remember that a smaller sit-down meal will be more seriously disrupted by a late arrival than a large drinks party.

Cancelling: if you have to cancel a party you should write or ring all those who have been invited to let them know.

Drinks: it is up to the hosts to decide what they serve according to the kind of party they are giving. Unless you have hired staff, you should make the choice of drinks simple if you are expecting a large number of guests.

Try to moderate your drinking at parties so that you do not disrupt the atmosphere or disturb other guests. Over drinking is more disruptive at a small sit down meal than at a larger gathering.

Food: whenever you serve alcoholic drinks, you should also serve food, even if it is just peanuts and crisps. If guests are invited for any length of time, something more substantial should be provided.

Leaving: some invitations – especially to pre-meal drinks parties – will indicate when guests are expected to leave. Invitations to balls may also indicate when guests should leave. At formal functions, guests should not leave before the guest of honour has left. At dinner parties, guests can leave once the coffee has been served but not before. If you stay on after other guests have left, make sure that you are not keeping your hosts up against their will. See **Dinner Parties** and **Parties and Entertaining** in Special Occasions.

pâté
Pâté is served with toast and butter, and the polite way of eating it is to break off a small piece of toast, butter it and then spread it with pâté.

peas
Peas should be eaten like other foods from the downturned tines of the fork. However, except for very formal meals, it is generally considered acceptable to turn the fork over to 'shovel' those last few, difficult-to-pin-down peas.

personal questions
If you want to ask someone a personal question, let him or her know that you will not mind if he or she is not prepared to answer. If someone asks you a question which you feel is too personal, tell that person that you would rather not answer.

pets
Pet owners should always ask before taking their pets to someone else's house. Once there, the pet should be kept well disciplined and any accidents should be cleared up immediately by the profusely apologetic owner. Pets should not be allowed onto other people's furniture even if they are allowed to do this at home.

You should never shy away from saying that you don't like or are allergic to animals; owners should respect this and take their pets away. Tell owners if you don't want their pets on your furniture or even in your house.

On the other hand, you may love all sorts of animals, but it is not a good idea to be over familiar with someone else's pet unless you know it well: boisterous games and teasing may irritate an animal, and could end in tears. You should never feed a pet titbits without asking its owner; many owners do not like their pets to learn to beg, and just one kindly meant titbit might teach the animal to beg from other guests.

Pets as gifts: you should always think very carefully before giving someone a pet as a gift. If the gift is for a child, check with his or her parents whether or not they approve of the idea. If you would like to give a pet to an adult, it is best to discuss the matter with him or her however much this will detract from the surprise.

See also **dogs (in public places)** in this section.

photographs (taking)
It is extremely rude to take someone's photograph without asking their permission, for example, if you are on holiday and want to take a photograph of some of the locals where you are staying, you should always ask them first.

pips (spitting out)
When you have to spit out pips or stones in your food, bring your spoon or fork up to your mouth, pop the stone onto it and then leave it on the side of your plate.

plates
Laying: the side plate is laid to the left-hand side of the place setting. Plates for the first course may be laid ready on the table

before guests sit down. They may be laid on top of the dinner plates to show off the dinner service, or the dinner plates may be kept warm in the oven until they are needed.

Paper plates: at large parties, especially less formal ones, it is quite acceptable to use paper plates. If guests are to stand up and eat off paper plates, you should serve food that does not need cutting up.

pointing
It is rude to point at people.

port
Passing: port should be served first to the guest of honour, to the right-hand side of the host; then it should be passed to the left, clockwise round the table. Even if you are not drinking port, make a point of passing it on every time it comes to you.

When to serve: port is served towards the end of a meal, either with or after the cheese course.

postcards
Postcards are an easy way of keeping in touch with friends, but they may not always be adequate for thank-you notes. If you are thanking someone for a gift or a special occasion you should really write a letter.

postponements
If you have to postpone any function you should send out notes to everyone who was invited to let them know. If the post-ponement happens at the last moment, you will have to contact them by telephone.

praise
As with compliments, if someone praises you for something you have done, it is polite to thank him or her for the praise. If you

are genuinely proud of what you have done, don't be falsely modest by saying 'it was nothing'.

prawns (unpeeled)
When you are served unpeeled prawns first pull off the tail, then ease the fleshy body away from the legs and shell, and finally tug it away from the head. Dip the prawn into the sauce, if provided, before eating. Do not lick your fingers but clean them on your napkin or, if there is one, rinse them first in the finger bowl.

pregnancy
It is customary for men and women to offer their seats to pregnant women on public transport. Women may behave and eat differently when they are pregnant, so when you invite a pregnant friend to stay or to a meal, check, for example, whether she needs a lot of sleep or whether she can't eat certain foods.

presents
You should always write promptly to thank someone for a present. The letter need not be long and it need not deal only with the gift, but it is polite to reiterate your thanks at the end of the letter. See **Correct Gifts** in Basic Rules.

privacy
Always respect other people's privacy, for example, knocking before going into someone's room or office, asking whether someone minds you dropping in to say hello, and respecting someone's wish not to discuss certain things.

public transport
When travelling on public transport you should always show consideration for your fellow travellers. For example: don't put your feet up on a seat next to someone; don't take up a seat with

your luggage; always give up your seat to an elderly or disabled person or a pregnant woman; don't make too much noise, for example, keep your personal stereo turned down; if someone falls asleep wake them when the train comes into a station, just in case it is the one they want.

pubs

Most pubs are usually divided into two distinct sections, the public bar and the saloon or lounge bar. The public bar is usually the place where pub games, such as darts or pool, are played, and the lounge is where people are more likely to sit. The attraction of a pub is that of a relaxed, informal and sociable atmosphere, however, there are a few generally accepted codes of behaviour.

Making sure that you buy your round of drinks is particularly important, and it is expected that each person in a group should take it in turns to buy the drinks. If you are planning to leave early you should make a point of buying a round early on. If you knock over someone else's drink you must offer to buy them another, however little may have been spilt. If you accept the offer of a drink from a stranger while standing at the bar, it is polite to at least talk to them for the time it takes to finish the drink.

If you are with a non-drinker you should not try to persistently encourage them to have a drink. If someone buys a non-drinker a drink, even when they have refused, it is acceptable for him or her not to drink it.

punctuality

It is polite to be as punctual as possible for all appointments. You should arrive within 20 minutes of the stated time on an invitation (there is more leeway with larger functions) and you should arrive a little in advance for interviews and other business meetings.

queuing

Queuing can be very frustrating especially if you are running late and if, as always seems to be the case, you feel you are in the slowest moving queue. But remember that everyone in the line is in the same situation as yourself and tolerate it with as good grace as you can manage.

Don't cramp the person immediately in front of you by edging your way closer and closer to them in the misguided belief that this will make the queue move more quickly. You will achieve little by sighing and tutting to show your impatience either with those ahead of you in the queue, or with the unfortunate person behind the counter who is trying to work under pressure. If you do demonstrate your impatience you will either fluster them, therefore making them less efficient, or annoy them so that they feel inclined to work slowly deliberately!

referees

A referee should be someone who knows you well enough to comment on your ability as an employee. Ideally, he or she should be a former employer; his or her opinion will then be more valid in the eyes of your prospective employer. If you are applying for many jobs and using a referee's name regularly, it is polite to let your referee know the names and addresses of all the companies that have been given his or her name.

references

Letters of reference should be relevant and truthful. If you are asked to write a reference for someone, but you feel you really cannot recommend him or her, it is better to decline to write the letter than to lie.

refusing drink

A guest may always refuse an alcoholic drink and ask for a soft drink instead. To reinforce a refusal, the guest should lay his or her hand across the glass briefly.

remarriage

Those who have been widowed can judge for themselves when they feel ready to remarry. The divorced may remarry when the decree absolute has been issued, but the Church of England, after discussing the matter, will offer only a service of blessing and not a full marriage service to divorcés. However, the Church of Scotland does allow divorced couples to remarry with a full marriage service, but the minister must agree first.

restaurants

Whether eating out formally or informally there are a few guidelines which you should bear in mind.

It should be clear at the time of the invitation who will be paying for a restaurant meal. If you agree to go out for a meal with friends you should share the bill. If you invite someone out for a meal, you should pay for it. Conversely, if you are invited out for a meal there should not be any need for you to offer to pay.

What you wear to a restaurant depends only to a small extent on the establishment itself: some very smart restaurants or the dining rooms of certain clubs and hotels may stipulate that men wear a tie or they may even require evening dress after 6 pm. In most cases, the choice is yours, and you should agree what to wear with the person or people you have invited for the meal so that no-one feels under– or overdressed.

If you have invited a friend or friends to a restaurant, you should always arrive a little early so that they do not have to wait for you.

When someone asks you out for a meal, some people would say that it is rude to choose either the cheapest or the most expensive dish on the menu.

When eating in a restaurant diners should observe the same courtesies as when invited to eat at someone else's house. They should also remember that they are not the only clients in the restaurant. You should also be especially attentive to the fact that other people may not like you to smoke while they are eating.

Waiting staff should always be treated courteously; they are professionals, not servants and their service will be better if you treat them as such.

You should not be embarrassed about complaining if you have a genuine reason to do so, on the other hand few problems that arise during the course of a restaurant meal warrant a real scene. If you would like to complain about something it is best to leave your table – therefore avoiding embarrassing your guest or guests – and talk to the waiting staff or the manager.

See also **Restaurant Meals** in Special Occasions.

rice

Rice should be eaten like other foods from the downturned tines of the fork. However, except for very formal meals, it is generally considered acceptable to turn the fork over to 'shovel' up the last few bits.

Royal Ascot

The Royal Enclosure at Ascot stipulates that men should wear morning dress, and ladies should wear skirts or dresses and that the crown of their heads should be covered.

royal functions

See **Formal and Royal Functions** in Special Occasions.

RSVP
This stands for *répondez s'il vous plaît*, and when written on an invitation means that you should reply to the person inviting you to say whether you will be coming or not.

sailing
Before you go check what clothes and equipment you may need, let your host know if you are inclined to seasickness or if you can't swim, and try to learn a few useful words because sailing boats have a vocabulary all their own.

saunas
Although having a sauna would seem to be one occasion which requires no etiquette, there are one or two things to bear in mind. You must not increase the steam without asking the other people in the sauna first. You should also use a towel to cover yourself, especially if the sauna is a mixed one.

Scottish formal dress
Scottish formal dress may be worn to any formal occasion, whether 'black tie', 'white tie' or morning dress is stipulated. The type of jacket worn with the kilt should be either a 'Prince Charlie' (made of black barathea with silver buttons), or a 'Montrose' (made of black velvet). The shirt should be a white evening shirt with a black bow tie or a lace jabot if you are wearing a Montrose. The shoes can be either heavy brogues or patent leather with cross-over straps, and the socks cream or dark. Never wear dress tartan.

scratching
It is impolite to scratch – certainly vigorously or for any length of time – in public.

seating plans

Some hosts like to display a copy of their seating plan so that guests know where they will be sitting. Guests should make a note of the seating plan and each man should take the lady on his right through to the table (the host will take the female guest of honour who should be seated on his right). See also **Dinner Parties** in Special Occasions.

secrets

If you confide in someone by giving them information that you would prefer them to keep to themselves, let your friend know that you are showing your trust in him or her by sharing this information, and that you don't want him or her to tell anyone else. If a friend confides in you, don't betray your friend's confidence by telling others what he or she has told you.

separation

If you know a couple who have separated, it is quite acceptable to remain in contact with both partners – especially if their separation was not acrimonious. You should not, however, invite both partners to the same function, or at least tell either of them who you are inviting to allow them time to refuse.

sexual harassment

If something you say, do or intimate seems to upset or offend the person it is addressed to, you should respect his or her wishes and stop immediately. If you are the 'victim' of such comments or actions, confront the person who is upsetting you. Let the offending person know that you do not like what he or she is doing, and warn him or her that you will speak to someone else about your feelings if you have to. In extreme cases you should refer the matter to an industrial tribunal.

shoes (removing)

You should only remove your shoes in a very informal situation, but if you are among close friends it is perfectly acceptable and is a sign that you are quite relaxed and at home. However, before doing so it is sensible to mentally check whether you have fresh socks on and that they are not full of holes.

shower parties

The North American custom of holding 'shower parties' is beginning to take on in the UK: friends are invited to, for example, a 'glass shower', and each guest brings an appropriate gift – such as a glass bowl.

shyness

If you meet a shy person or someone who seems uncommunicative, be patient with him or her and tolerant of his or her brief replies. Try to ask questions that need more than a yes or no answer so that the person is drawn out.

If you are very shy, try not to worry about it before meeting other people. The more you think about it, the more of a handicap your shyness will be. If someone starts a conversation with you, make a concerted effort to give full answers to their questions rather than just saying yes or no; this will make it easier for them to continue talking to you, which should help build your confidence.

side plates

Side plates should be laid to the left-hand side of the place setting.

sitting at table

When sitting at table for a meal you should sit upright with your hands either in your lap or resting lightly on the table. Don't put your elbows on the table: you might tip the table and you will make it difficult for those on either side of you to talk to each other.

small talk

Small talk – conversation about trivial matters such as the weather – is the safest way of making conversation with people you have just met. It is, however, shallow and bland; if you want to make an impression on someone or to get to know someone better you should break away from small talk and address more interesting or even controversial topics. See also **conversation** in this section.

smoking

Smoking is increasingly a contentious and unacceptable habit in many social situations. It is therefore important to show consideration and follow some simple guidelines.

Before lighting a cigarette, cigar or pipe, you should consider the circumstances carefully. If you are in a public place, you should check first for 'No Smoking' signs and, if applicable, move to a designated smoking area. Check also that there is an ashtray close at hand.

Always ask people with you or nearby whether they mind you smoking, especially if you are in a confined space or if anyone is eating. If someone says that they do mind you should not smoke.

You should make a particular point of asking if you are in the home, office or car of a non-smoker. People who live in a smoke-free environment are especially sensitive to the lingering smell of tobacco smoke. It would be most discourteous to argue if they asked you not to smoke.

Once you have established that no-one minds you smoking, it is polite to offer cigarettes to your companions. It is also polite to offer a light to anyone with an unlit cigarette.

snails
When snails are served in their shells a special pair of tongs and a little pick or two-tined fork will be provided. The tongs are used to hold the shell steady while prying the flesh out with either the pick or the fork.

sneezing
It is impossible to stop yourself sneezing and it is, therefore, advisable to have a handkerchief with you at all times in case you sneeze. When you sneeze you should cover you nose with your handkerchief or at least your hand. If you need to keep a sneeze quiet – for example, during a performance – try pinching your nostrils hard as you sneeze.

sniffing
It is rude and often unpleasant to sniff. You should carry a hand-kerchief with you at all times, and blow your nose rather than sniffing. If you do not have a handkerchief it is better to ask someone for a tissue, or even some lavatory paper, than to sniff.

soup
When drinking soup the spoon should be held across the body, the end of its handle held down onto the first two fingers by the flat of the thumb. When scooping the soup, place the spoon into bowl at the edge nearest to you, then scoop the spoon through the soup away from the body not towards it. Bring the spoon to your mouth but do not put it in, the soup should be poured from the side of the spoon into your mouth, and certainly not sucked. As you finish your soup, tip the bowl away from the body, not towards it, to spoon up the last of the soup. If your soup is served in a large bowl (plates), leave the spoon in it when you have finished; if it is served in small cups on saucers, leave the spoon on the saucer.

spaghetti
When eating spaghetti push your fork into it and pull free some of the strands, then twirl the fork round with the tines pressing against the plate. Lift the fork up from the plate and make sure that you only have a few, short pieces hanging down. If, however, you do not feel adept enough to eat spaghetti this way, use a spoon to hold it in place while you twist the fork around.

spitting
Spitting is very unattractive and unhygienic, and many people find it offensive. Do not spit in front of other people.

spoons
See **cutlery** in this section.

stag parties
There is no need for a bridegroom to have a stag party although it is a popular tradition. The party – which may be anything from a simple meal to a lavish weekend away – is best held a few days before the wedding so that the groom has time to recover. Stag parties are traditionally organized by the best man.

staring
It is rude to stare. Adults should resist the temptation to stare at other people, and children should be taught not to stare.

step-children
As with any children, the best way to deal with step-children is to treat them in as adult a way as possible. Don't patronize or spoil them and certainly don't try to force any intimacy or show of affection with them; step-children may have powerful feelings of resentment towards their step-parent and should be allowed to overcome these feelings in their own time.

step-parents
Very young children may take easily to calling their step-parents mummy or daddy, although this can cause hurt if their true mother or father is still alive. It is often best for step-children to use their step-parents' first names.

sunglasses
Unless you are on a beach it is quite off-putting and rude to keep your sunglasses on when talking to someone, especially if you don't know them that well. You should always remove your sunglasses when you come indoors.

supermarket checkouts
In a busy supermarket it is important to keep your patience and to have degree of resignation. However, it is helpful to make sure that you are in the correct line, and not in the 'express' till with a trolley piled high with shopping. If you do feel that you have queued for far too long, don't complain to the person on the till, take your complaint to the manager or supervisor instead.

swearing
It is impolite to swear or to blaspheme, and you should avoid swearing at any time but should be especially careful in front of people you respect or are trying to impress. You should never swear in front of children.

tablecloths
It is up to the hosts to decide whether or not they use a tablecloth for a lunch or dinner party. A tablecloth may be a useful way of disguising an unattractive table or a number of tables that have been put together. White damask tablecloths are elegant accessories for formal meals.

table decorations
Many hosts like to have some form of table decoration for lunch
and dinner parties. Whether you choose a fresh or dried flower
arrangement, a china or silver ornament, make sure that the
table decoration is not so wide that it interferes with anyone's
place setting, nor so high that it blocks guests' view of each
other.

table manners
This subject is comprehensively dealt with in the **Table Manners** section in Basic Rules. However, here are a few general
rules of behaviour: always compliment the host on the food;
make sure you talk to both your neighbours during the meal;
always ask for something (such as the salt), and never stretch
across the table for it; never speak with your mouth full, the best
way to avoid this is to make sure that you only take small
amounts of food at a time; when speaking never use your cutlery
to emphasize what you are saying; don't lick your fingers, use
your napkin or the finger bowl if one is provided.

table mats
There is no need to use table mats for a meal unless you want to
protect the table from hot plates and serving dishes. If you use a
tablecloth but still want to protect the table from hot plates, the
mats are usually put under the cloth.

taxis
If you are trying to hail a taxi, you should not be shy of waving
your arm above your head. There is little point in calling,
though, because the driver is very unlikely to hear you. If two
people hail a taxi at the same time, the driver will go to the
person he or she sees first. You should not take a taxi if you know
that someone else was hailing it first. A taxi is under no obli-

gation to stop when you hail it, but if a taxi driver does respond to your hailing, he or she is obliged to take you to your destination.

It is customary to tip taxi drivers 10 or 15% of the fare.

tea

If you are invited to tea you may be being offered a hot refreshing drink with a couple of biscuits; a full, traditional afternoon tea with cucumber sandwiches and cake; or an early evening meal. It is best to clarify any ambiguity before accepting.

After a meal: tea is becoming an increasingly popular alternative to coffee after a meal. Good hosts should offer it to their guests as a matter of course.

Serving: if tea is being poured from a pot and it is taken with milk, the milk is usually put into the cup or mug first.

telephone

Introducing oneself on: when you telephone someone you have not met it is very important to let him or her know who you are. Give him or her your name – and, if relevant, the name of your company – and explain why you are calling and/or who gave you his or her name.

Inviting by: invitations for casual or impromptu functions may be made by telephone, but invitations for more formal functions should be made in writing. The advantage of telephone invitations is that they can be made nearer the time of the function because they usually get an immediate answer. Some hosts like to send out a written invitation once a telephone invitation has been accepted; they may cross out the letters RSVP and substitute the letters PM (*Pour Mémoire* – as a reminder).

Replying by: if an invitation gives a telephone number next to the letters RSVP, you should reply by telephone; otherwise you should reply in writing.

Thanking on: you should only really thank people for the most minor things on the telephone: a casual drinks party or a light meal offered on the spur of the moment. More momentous occasions and gifts deserve a letter of thanks.

See also **Telephone Etiquette** in Basic Rules.

temper

Curbing: if you are angered by something that someone has done or are in a bad mood, you should curb your temper for the sake of those around you. Make an effort to join in the conversation wholeheartedly and cheerfully. If the cause of your anger is another person you may ask to speak to them privately to sort out your differences without disturbing or embarrassing other people.

Dealing with: if someone is in a bad mood, try to coax him or her out of the mood by incorporating him or her in the conversation, but do not force or rush this process – that might irritate him or her further. If you have angered someone, try to use the same tactics unless it is quite obvious that he or she will not be mollified. In this case, you should speak to him or her privately to sort out your differences without disturbing or embarrassing other people.

tennis

Poor manners on the tennis court can easily damage friendships, even – or perhaps especially – in casual games without umpires. If the players are in any doubt about whether a ball was in or not, they should simply play the point again rather than arguing.

In doubles matches, partners should discuss whether they intend to work the sides of the court or the front and the back; once established, they should respect each other's 'territory' and apologize if they infringe on it.

Some tennis clubs or even the owners of private courts like players to wear full tennis whites on their courts. If you are joining a tennis club, going to a tennis party, or borrowing someone's court, check whether you should wear tennis whites.

thank-you letters
See **letters** in this section.

thank-yous
Acknowledging: when someone thanks-you verbally for something, it is polite to acknowledge their thanks by saying something like it's a 'pleasure'.

Saying: whenever someone gives you something, entertains you or goes to any trouble on your behalf, you should always thank him or her in person immediately. You may follow this up by telephoning or writing to reiterate your thanks.

tickets
Booking: anyone organizing a trip to, for example, the theatre, should avoid disappointment by booking tickets in advance. This can usually be done by going to the box office in person or by making a credit card booking over the telephone.

Paying for: when someone organizes a party of friends to attend, for example, a concert, he or she should make it clear whether the other members of the party are being invited as guests – in which case they are not expected to pay for their tickets – or if they are expected to pay for their tickets. Either way, it is usually most convenient for one person to pay for all the tickets in the first place, whether or not he or she is to be reimbursed by the others later.

tipping
See **Tipping** in Basic Rules.

toastmaster

At formal functions there may be a master of ceremonies or toastmaster present to introduce the speakers, and to announce the toasts after they have been proposed by the speakers.

toasts

After a meal: a number of speakers may be called upon to speak and propose toasts after formal or celebratory meals. If you have to propose a toast, you should have been provided with something to drink, and you should say: 'I would like to propose a toast to [for example] the chairman of the board, Mr Horden.' You then raise your glass and just repeat the words 'Mr Horden'; your listeners should stand, raise their glasses and say these words with you, before taking a sip from their drinks.

At engagement parties: if a couple or one of their families hold an engagement party, it is customary for one of the parents, or a close friend, to propose a toast to the engaged couple. The toast may be drunk in whatever drink is available at the party; some families like to provide champagne, but wine, spirits or beer are equally acceptable.

At christening parties: if a party is held after a christening, it is customary for one of the godparents to propose a toast to the newly christened baby. The toast may be drunk in whatever drink is available at the party; some families like to provide champagne, but wine or even a cup of tea are equally acceptable.

At wedding receptions: at most wedding receptions, three toasts are made, one by each of the speakers. The first speaker, usually the father of the bride, proposes a toast to the newly married couple. The groom then responds on behalf of his wife and himself; he ends his speech by proposing a toast to the bridesmaids and any flower girls or pageboys. The best man thanks the groom on behalf of the bridesmaids, flowert girls and pageboys, and concludes his speech with a final toast to the bride and groom.

See also **loyal and patriotic toasts** in this section.

toothbrushes

Never use someone else's toothbrush if you happen to be staying somewhere and have forgotten your own. If you ask, it is very likely that your host will have a spare, new one.

toothpicks

Toothpicks are very occasionally provided on the table with foods that are inclined to cling to the teeth. In this case it is acceptable to use a toothpick at the table so long as the mouth is masked with a hand. If you like to use a toothpick regularly, you should do so in private.

topless sunbathing

If you wish to sunbathe topless you should always keep to beaches where it is acceptable. In many countries topless sunbathing is unacceptable and you may run the risk of at least seriously offending people, if not actually breaking the law.

umbrellas

When using an umbrella always show consideration for other people, especially on crowded city pavements. Hold it so that you can see other people coming and when necessary be prepared to raise it above someone or move it to the side so that you can pass without clashing. It is not only rude but dangerous to barge through people with an umbrella.

If you are walking with someone who has no umbrella you must offer to share, and make sure you hold it so that you both get at least some protection. When entering anywhere, such as a shop, always shake out your umbrella first, and, if provided, look for a stand to leave it in.

uninvited guests
See **guests** in this section.

ushers
In a big church wedding it may be necessary to have ushers to distribute service sheets, to ensure that the correct number of pews are reserved for the immediate families of the bride and groom, and to show guests to their seats. Those who are chosen as ushers should ideally know some relations and friends of the bride and/or groom. If an usher does not recognize a guest, he should ask 'bride or groom?': guests who are friends of the bride should be seated to the left of the aisle as one looks at the altar, and friends of the groom to the right.

veils
Funerals: traditionally women in deep mourning wore veils. This custom has now been reduced to the fact that a woman in mourning may choose to wear a veil with or without a hat at a funeral or cremation service. There is no need to wear a veil, and before choosing to wear one a woman should consider how tearful she is likely to be during the service; a veil can make it more difficult to deal with tears quickly and discreetly.

Weddings: at a white church wedding the bride traditionally wears a veil. There is no need for the bride to wear a veil, although many still choose to. If the bride is wearing a veil it should be lifted – probably with the help of the chief bridesmaid – as the marriage ceremony begins.

visits

Arrival time: if you have been invited to visit someone, he or she should let you know when to arrive. If you drop in on someone, it is best not to do so before 10 in the morning, or after 6 in the evening.

Taking a present: when you visit someone, especially if you have been invited to stay for any length of time or if the person you are visiting is sick, it is polite to take a gift of some sort. A box of chocolates or some other confectionery, flowers or a plant, perhaps a bottle of drink or some exotic fruit; all of these may be suitable gifts according to the circumstances.

To mothers with new babies: if you are visiting a mother with a new baby, you should always check in advance when would be a good time to call. It is polite to take a small gift for the baby, such as a toy or an article of clothing. The mother will probably be tired so you should not stay more than an hour unless she insists that you do.

To the elderly: the elderly, especially those who live alone, usually welcome visitors. Before visiting elderly people you should check when would be a good time; you would not, for example, want to disturb them at a time when they like to rest. Even though you are technically the guest, you may want to help to prepare a cup of tea or a light meal, you may even offer to do some little chores; this obviously depends on how active and able your elderly friend is. The elderly can get tired very suddenly, so you should check for signs of tiredness and should not stay for more than an hour unless he or she insists you do.

To the sick: see **Visiting the Sick** in Special Occasions.

When to leave: if you have been invited to visit someone, he or she will usually have given some indication of when you should leave (if, for example, you have been invited for a fairly formal meal, you should leave shortly after the meal is finished). If you visit someone – such as an elderly person – who is likely to tire easily, check for signs of tiredness and leave within an hour of your arrival. If you drop in on someone uninvited, you should also leave within an hour of your arrival. In any circumstances your host may press you to stay on in which case you must judge carefully when it would be appropriate to leave.

vomiting

If you feel that you are going to vomit, you should make every effort to get to a bathroom immediately. If this is not possible you should find a corner where you can be ill as discreetly as possible. It goes without saying that, if you are ill in someone else's home, you should apologize profusely and should help to clear up unless you are too ill to do so. You should never talk about vomiting.

waiting staff

When hailing waiting staff you should never whistle, call or snap your fingers across the room. You should attract their attention by catching their eye, raising your hand or saying 'excuse me' as they pass near you. If the waiter or waitress still fails to come over to your table, go over and tell the person firmly that you have been calling for some time.

walking home at night

Men should always be aware that at night a woman on her own may be anxious of a man walking behind her. It is considerate to put her mind at rest by crossing to the other side of the street, or by walking quickly past and away from her.

water

Water should always be offered as an alternative to wine during a meal. You may choose to serve mineral water or fresh tap water in a jug, and you may add some ice cubes and/or a few slices of lemon or lime.

wedding rings
A wedding ring is usually a plain gold band, though many different designs are available. The groom always gives his bride a ring, but a bride may also give a ring in exchange.

weddings
See **Weddings** in Special Occasions.

white tie
This formal dress, also known as full evening dress, comprises black tail coat and trousers, a stiff-fronted shirt with a wing collar and studs, and a matching white bow tie and waistcoat. Shoes should be patent leather Oxfords. 'White tie' is usually only worn at very formal occasions. See also **black tie** in this section and **Correct Clothes** in Basic Rules.

widows (addressing)
A widow is addressed using her husband's name, for example Mrs Robert Mason.

wills
A will need not be a long and complicated document, but it is a great help to the family of the bereaved. The estate of someone who dies without leaving a will is divided according to the intestacy laws. These laws aim to distribute an estate according to the deceased's presumed wish that he or she would want the property to benefit their closest relatives. These laws, however, were written many years ago and society has changed considerably, for instance more people now own their own homes, and there is more divorce, remarriage and cohabitation. In consequence,

these laws formulated in a past social context when applied in today's may seem arbitrary and clumsy. So the best thing to do is to avoid this situation by making a will.

Solicitors can advise you how to make a will, and can draw one up for you. Many people first make a will when they get married or when they have children, and they may change their will periodically during their lives.

The truly thoughtful give some idea in their will of what sort of funeral arrangements they would like, and they may leave money specifically to cover for these arrangements. If you would like your will to include rather eccentric instructions for your burial, take the precaution of checking how much it will all cost and how easily it can be arranged. The next of kin are actually not legally bound to obey these burial instructions.

wind (breaking)
The degree of embarrassment that results from involuntary and unexpected wind breaking increases with the formality of the occasion. Although the perpetrator is usually as surprised as anyone else, there is still a sense of guilt of having given offence and of abusing the hospitality of the host. If you are at a dinner party with friends it may be easily shrugged off with a laugh, but at a formal event the only recourse is to act as though it never happened. It is not polite, and at the wrong occasion not funny, to look at someone else accusingly.

windows (opening)
In any public place or situation you should always ask other people first before opening or shutting a window, especially on trains and buses.

wine
As a gift: as with any kind of drink, wine usually makes a welcome gift. You may choose to give one bottle of very special wine

or a case – or half case – of more everyday wine. If you take a bottle of wine as a gift for the hosts of a dinner or lunch party, you should not expect it to be drunk during the course of the meal as your hosts will almost certainly have bought wine to go with the meal.

With a meal: ideally, there should be a different wine chosen to go with each course of a meal, and there should be a different glass for each wine. Many hosts will offer simply a choice of red or white wine throughout the meal or they may have chosen just one wine that complements all of the courses.

However, there are a few general guidelines concerning what type of wine should accompany different foods: sherry is usually drunk with soup; dry white wines with shellfish and fish; rich, heavy red wines with red meat and game; lighter reds with other red meat, such as lamb; light reds, medium whites or rosé with white meat; sweet, dessert wines or champagne with puddings.

women

Addressing: a woman may be addressed as Miss, Ms or Mrs, or by any other title she may have, such as Lady or Doctor. Before addressing a letter to a woman you should try to discover how she likes to be addressed. In social correspondence, such as invitations, married and widowed women are addressed using their husband's name, for example Mrs Robert Mason. Divorced women are addressed using their own first name, for example Mrs Alison Mason.

Dress for formal functions: the clothes that a woman should wear for a formal function depend on the function itself and on the time of day. During the day a woman should wear a smart suit or dress, with a hat and gloves if she chooses. At an evening function she should wear a full– or calf-length dress or skirt, with gloves.

Exposing legs: the fashionable height for hemlines alters regularly, but whatever the fashion a woman should think before wearing a very short skirt. Very short skirts are not advisable for job interviews, for funerals and cremations or for very formal functions. Women are not admitted into the Stewards' Enclosure at the Henley Royal Regatta if they are wearing above knee-length skirts.

Exposing shoulders: off-the-shoulder dresses may be worn on most occasions; but some people disapprove of bare shoulders in church (even for weddings). At very formal functions, women may be expected to keep their shoulders covered up unless there is to be dancing, in which case off-the-shoulder dresses are acceptable.

work relationships
See **Office Etiquette** in Basic Rules.

yawning
It is rude to yawn in public. If you feel the need to yawn, you should cover your mouth with your hand and, if someone sees you yawn, you should apologize.

FORMS OF ADDRESS

The information is given in the following way:
Addressing: how to address the person in conversation (this section is omitted if the person is simply addressed by his or her name).
Addressing envelope: how to address an envelope to the person
Salutation: how to open a letter to the person.
Introducing: how to introduce the person to someone else.

ROYALTY
The Queen
Addressing: Your Majesty, thereafter 'Ma'am'
Addressing envelope: The Private Secretary to Her Majesty the Queen
Salutation: Dear Sir (or Madam if the Private Secretary is a woman)
Introducing: Her Majesty the Queen

The Duke of Edinburgh
Addressing: Your Royal Highness, therefater 'Sir'
Addressing envelope: The Private Secretary to His Royal Highness the Duke of Edinburgh
Salutation: Dear Sir (or Madam if the Private Secretary is a woman)
Introducing: His Royal Highness, Prince Philip, Duke of Edinburgh

FORMS OF ADDRESS

Royal Princes and Princesses
Addressing: Your Royal Highness, thereafter 'Sir/Ma'am'
Addressing envelope: His/Her Royal Highness, The Prince/Princess first name
Salutation: Your Royal Highness
Introducing: His/Her Royal Highness [then full title]

Royal Dukes and Duchesses
Addressing: Your Royal Highness, thereafter 'Sir/Ma'am'
Addressing envelope: His/Her Royal Highness, The Duke/Duchess of place name
Salutation: Your Royal Highness
Introducing: His/Her Royal Highness [then full title]

ARISTOCRACY
Dukes and Duchesses
Addressing: Duke/Duchess
Addressing envelope; The Duke/Duchess of [place name]
Salutation: Dear Duke/Duchess
Introducing: The Duke/Duchess of [place name]

Earls and Countesses
Addressing: Lord/Lady [place name]
Addressing envelope: The Earl/Countess of [place name]
Salutation: Dear Lord/Lady [place name]
Introducing: Lord/Lady [place name]

Barons and their wives
Addressing: Sir/Lady first [name and place name]
Addressing envelope: The Lord/Lady [place name]
Salutation: Dear Lord/Lady [place name]
Introducing: Lord/Lady [place name]

Honourables (children of aristocracy)
Addressing: Mr/Miss [surname]
Addressing envelope: The Honourable (or The Hon.) [full name]
Salutation: Dear Mr/Miss [surname]
(The married daughter of an aristocrat retains the title Honourable, becoming The Hon. Mrs husband's name)

Knights and their wives
Addressing: Sir [first name]; Lady [surname]
Addressing envelope: Sir/Lady [full name]
Salutation: Dear Sir [first name]; Lady [surname]
Introducing: Sir/Lady [full name]

Dames
Addressing: Dame [first name]
Addressing envelope: Dame [full name]
Salutation: Dear [full name]
Introducing: Dame [full name]

GOVERNMENT MINISTERS
The Prime Minister
Addressing: by office or name
Addressing envelope: The Rt Hon [full name] MP
Salutation: Dear Prime Minister
Introducing: by office or name

The Chancellor of the Exchequer
Addressing: as 'Chancellor' or by name
Addressing envelope: The Rt Hon [full name] MP
Salutation: Dear Chancellor
Introducing: by office or name

FORMS OF ADDRESS

Secretaries of State
Addressing: by office or name
Addressing envelope: The Rt. Hon. [full name], PC, MP or by appointment only, e.g. The Foreign Secretary
Salutation: Dear Secretary of State or Dear [appointment]
Introducing: by office or name

Ministers
Addressing: Minister or Mr [surname]
Addressing envelope: [full name], Esq., MP or by appointment
Salutation: Dear Minister
Introducing: Mr [surname]

Members of Parliament
Addressing: Mr [surname]
Addressing envelope: [full name] Esq., MP
Salutation: Dear Mr [surname]
Introducing: Mr [surname]

THE CLERGY – CHURCH OF ENGLAND
Archbishops
Addressing: Archbishop
Addressing envelope: The Most Reverend and Rt. Hon., the Lord Archbishop of [place name]
Salutation: Dear Archbishop
Introducing: The Archbishop of [place name]

Bishops
Addressing: Bishop
Addressing envelope: The Right Reverend the Lord Bishop of [place name]
Salutation: Dear Bishop
Introducing: The Bishop of [place name]

Deans
Addressing: Dean
Addressing envelope: The Very Reverend the Dean of [place name]
Salutation: Dear Dean or Dear Mr Dean
Introducing: The Dean of [place name]

Archdeacons
Addressing: Archdeacon
Addressing envelope: The Venerable the Archdeacon of [place name]
Salutation: Dear Archdeacon or Dear Mr Archdeacon

Introducing: The Archdeacon of [place name]

Vicars and Rectors
Addressing: Vicar or rector
Addressing envelope: The Reverend [full name]
Salutation: Dear Mr [surname]; Dear Father [surname]
Introducing: Mr or Father [surname]

THE ROMAN CATHOLIC CHURCH
The Pope
Addressing: Your Holiness
Addressing envelope: His Holiness the Pope
Salutation: Your Holiness or Most Holy Father
Introducing: His Holiness the Pope

Cardinals
Addressing: Your Eminence or Cardinal [surname]
Addressing envelope: His Eminence the Cardinal Archbishop of [place name]; or (if not an archbishop) His Eminence Cardinal [surname]

FORMS OF ADDRESS

Salutation: Dear Cardinal [surname] or Your eminence
Introducing: His Eminence Cardinal [surname] or Cardinal
[surname]

Archbishops
Addressing: Your Grace or Archbishop [surname]
Addressing envelope: His Grace the Archbishop of [place name]
Salutation: Dear Archbishop [surname] or Your Grace

Introducing: His Grace the Archbishop of [surname] or
Archbishop [surname]

Bishops
Addressing: My Lord or Bishop [surname]
Addressing envelope: The right Reverend [full name], Bishop of
[place name]
Salutation: My Lord Bishop or Dear Bishop [surname]
Introducing: Bishop [surname] of [place name] or His Lordship
Bishop [surname] of [place name]

Monsignors
Addressing: Monsignor [surname]
Addressing envelope: The Reverend Monsignor [full name] or
The Reverend Monsignor
Salutation: Dear Monsignor [surname]
Introducing: Monsignor [surname]

CHURCH OF SCOTLAND
Ministers
Addressing: Mr/Mrs [surname]
Addressing envelope: The Reverend [full name]
Salutation: Dear Mr/Mrs [surname] or Dear Minister
Introducing: Mr/Mrs [surname]

JEWISH
The Chief Rabbi
Addressing: Chief Rabbi
Addressing envelope: The Chief Rabbi Dr [full name]
Salutation: Dear Chief Rabbi
Introducing: Chief Rabbi

Rabbis
Addressing: Rabbi [surname] or Dr if applicable
Addressing envelope: Rabbi [full name]
Salutation: Dear Rabbi [surname] or Dr if applicable
Introducing: Rabbi [surname]

LEGAL DIGNITARIES
The Lord Chancellor
Addressing: Lord Chancellor
Addressing envelope: The Rt. Hon., [full peerage title], The Lord Chancellor
Salutation: Dear Lord Chancellor or My Lord
Introducing: The Lord Chancellor

The Lord Chief Justice
Addressing: Lord Chief Justice
Addressing envelope: The Rt. Hon., The Lord Chief Justice of England, PC
Salutation: Dear Lord Chief Justice or My Lord
Introducing: The Lord Chief Justice
(PC means that he is a member of the Privy Council)

Lord Justice-General (of Scotland)
Addressing: Lord Justice-General
Addressing envelope: The Rt. Hon., The Lord Justice-General, PC
Salutation: Dear Justice-General or My Lord

FORMS OF ADDRESS

Introducing: Lord Justice-General

Master of the Rolls
Addressing: Master of the Rolls
Addressing envelope: The Master of the Rolls
Salutation: Dear Master of the Rolls
Introducing: The Master of the Rolls

High Court Judges
Addressing: My Lord (in court), Sir [first name]; Dame [first name]
Addressing envelope: The Hon. Mr/Mrs Justice [surname]
Salutation: Dear Judge/Madam
Introducing: Mr/Mrs Justice [surname] or Sir [full name]

Circuit Court Judges
Addressing: Your Honour (in court), Judge [surname]
Addressing envelope: His/Her Honour Judge [surname]
Salutation: (Dear) Sir/Madam
Introducing: Judge [surname]

Queen's Counsel
Addressing: Mr [surname]
Addressing envelope: [full name], Esq. QC /Mrs [surname], QC
Salutation: Dear Mr/Mrs [surname]
Introducing: Mr/Mrs [surname]

LOCAL GOVERNMENT/CIVIC OFFICIALS
Lord or Lady Mayoress
Addressing: My Lord/Lady Mayor/Mayoress
Addressing envelope: The Right Worshipful the Lord Mayor of [place name]/The Lady Mayoress of [place name]: except for

London, York, Belfast and Cardiff, which is The Rt. Hon. the Lord Mayor of [place name]
Salutation: Mr Lord Mayor (formal), Dear Lord Mayor (social); My Lady Mayoress (formal), Dear Lady Mayoress (social)
Introducing: by office alone or office with name

Mayors and Mayoresses
Addressing: Mr Mayor/Madam Mayoress
Addressing: Your Worship (subsequently Mr Mayor/Madam Mayoress)
Addressing envelope: The Right Worshipful the Mayor/Mayoress of [place name]
Salutation: Sir/Madam
Introducing: by office alone or office with name

Councillors
Addressing: Councillor Mr/Mrs/rank [surname]
Addressing envelope: Councillor Mr/Mrs/rank [full name]
Salutation: Dear Councillor
Introducing: Councillor Mr/Mrs/rank [full name]

ORDINARY PEOPLE
Married Women
Addressing: Mrs [married surname]
Addressing envelope: Mrs [first and surname]
Salutation: Dear Mrs [married surname]
Introducing: Mrs [married surname]

Daughters
Addressing: Miss [surname]
Addressing envelope: Miss [first and surname]; the eldest daughter may be just Miss [surname]

FORMS OF ADDRESS

Salutation: Dear Miss [surname]
Introducing: Miss [surname]

Widows
Addressing: Mrs [married surname]
Addressing envelope: Mrs [husbands first and surname]
Salutation: Dear Mrs [married surname]
Introducing: Mrs [married surname]

Divorcées
Addressing: Mrs [married surname]
Addressing envelope: Mrs [own first name, married surname]
Salutation: Dear Mrs [married surname]
Introducing: Mrs [married surname]

COLLINS POCKET REFERENCE

Other titles in the Pocket Reference series:

Letter Writing
A practical guide for anyone who needs to write letters,
whether for business or pleasure

Speaking in Public
A guide to speaking with confidence, whatever the occasion

Weddings
How to plan and organize a wedding, from the engagement
to the honeymoon

Ready Reference
A unique compendium of information on measurements,
symbols, codes and abbreviations

What Happened When?
A fascinating source of information for thousands of
dates and events

Card Games
A guide to the rules and strategies of play
for a wide selection of card games

(All titles £4.99)

COLLINS POCKET REFERENCE

Women's Health

Accessible, quick-reference A-Z guide to the medical
conditions which affect women of all ages

Prescription Drugs

Clear, uncomplicated explanations of prescription drugs
and their actions

Driving Skills

Advice and information on all the skills required by
the Driving Test

Office Organizer

A handy guide to all office practices, from ordering
stationery to chairing a meeting

Scottish Surnames

A guide to the family names of Scotland

(All above titles £4.99)

Clans and Tartans

The histories and tartans of over 130 clans

(£6.99)